2011 WORLD SERIES

THE YEAR
OF THE
St. Louis
Cardinals ™

CELEBRATING THE 2011
WORLD SERIES® CHAMPIONS

LIBRARY AND ARCHIVES CANADA CATALOGUING IN PUBLICATION

The Year of the St. Louis Cardinals: Celebrating the 2011 World Series Champions / Major League Baseball.

ISBN 978-0-7710-5725-0

1. St. Louis Cardinals (Baseball team). 2. World Series (Baseball) (2011). I. Major League Baseball (Organization)

GV875.S3Y32 2011   796.357'640977866   C2011-907260-2

We acknowledge the financial support of the Government of Canada through the Book Publishing Industry Development Program and that of the Government of Ontario through the Ontario Media Development Corporation's Ontario Book Initiative. We further acknowledge the support of the Canada Council for the Arts and the Ontario Arts Council for our publishing program.

Published simultaneously in the United States of America by McClelland & Stewart Ltd., P.O. Box 1030, Plattsburgh, New York 12901

Major League Baseball trademarks and copyrights are used with permission of Major League Baseball Properties, Inc.

Library of Congress Control Number: 2011918977
Printed and bound in the United States of America

Fenn/McClelland & Stewart Ltd.
75 Sherbourne Street
Toronto, Ontario
M5A 2P9
www.mcclelland.com

2011 WORLD SERIES

THE YEAR OF THE St. Louis Cardinals

CELEBRATING THE 2011 WORLD SERIES® CHAMPIONS

FENN
M&S

CONTENTS

ASK A MAJOR Leaguer — any Major Leaguer — what his idea of the perfect season is, and you can be certain that he'll include a World Series title in the ideal scenario. With all of the personal accolades available for the taking, the Commissioner's Trophy is still the top prize for players, coaches and executives alike.

The 2011 edition of the Fall Classic featured two teams with plenty of offensive firepower. The St. Louis Cardinals entered the contest having gone five years between World Series appearances, unlike their counterparts, the Texas Rangers, who were taking part in their second consecutive World Series but were still seeking the franchise's first championship. While the Cardinals' come-from-behind run to the playoffs was certainly memorable, the thing that gets a team immortalized is a World Series title.

"When this club gets together years from now, they will go, 'Hey, remember what we did?'" said Cardinals Manager Tony La Russa, who announced his retirement from baseball on Oct. 31, concluding a career that saw him finish third all time in wins.

What unfolded in St. Louis and Texas during the 2011 World Series was a sequence of thrilling games; contests being decided in final at-bats and wielding historic offensive performances. What it all adds up to is a truly classic Series, the best seen in at least a decade since the back-to-back, iconic Fall Classics of 2001 and '02.

From Albert Pujols joining the Babe and Mr. October in the record books to MVP David Freese's clutch hitting; from Chris Carpenter's strong pitching to the happy ending that perfectly framed the club's late-season surge, the Cardinals' against-all-odds run to the title had plenty of drama. Capturing it all — every pitch, every swing, every momentous hit or defensive play — were MLB editors and photographers, preserving the 2011 Fall Classic as stories and images that will be forever emblazoned in the memories of those who took in the Series, who relished every out and every dramatic momentum swing. This year's Fall Classic was another reminder of the joy that comes with watching baseball, and although no single quote or image could ever truly capture the breadth of emotion felt by players and fans at that moment, the stories they do tell serve as a reminder of a landmark event.

ASSEMBLING THE PIECES

TO DISTINGUISH BETWEEN this era of Cardinals success and everything that came before it, there is simply B.A. (Before Albert) and A.A. (After Albert). Albert Pujols, who was drafted by the Cardinals in 1999 and made his Big League debut in 2001, is the longest-tenured player on the roster. Through all of the player turnover that the team has experienced since he joined the club, there has been John Mozeliak. The 42-year-old joined the Cardinals' organization in 1995 as an assistant in the scouting department and later spent five years as assistant GM under Walt Jocketty before being hired as the general manager on Oct. 30, 2007. Be it through the draft, free agency or trade, Mozeliak has helped field a winning club nearly every season. Since 2000, St. Louis has had just one losing year, when the club went 78-84 in 2007, while making eight trips to the postseason and winning two championships.

Draft

Mitchell Boggs – 5th round, 2005
Adron Chambers – 38th round, 2007
Allen Craig – 8th round, 2006
Daniel Descalso – 3rd round, 2007
Jaime Garcia – 22nd round, 2005
Tyler Greene – 1st round, 2005
Jon Jay – 2nd round, 2006
Lance Lynn – 1st round, 2008
Kyle McClellan – 25th round, 2002
Yadier Molina – 4th round, 2000
Jason Motte – 19th round, 2003
Albert Pujols – 13th round, 1999
Skip Schumaker – 5th round, 2001

Free Agency

Lance Berkman – 1 year/$8M (2011)
Chris Carpenter – 5 years/$62.5M
Matt Holliday – 7 years/$120M, plus option (2010)
Gerald Laird – 1 year/$1.1M (2011)
Kyle Lohse – 4 years/$41M (2009)
Nick Punto – 1 year/$750K (2011)
Arthur Rhodes – 1 year/$3.9M, plus option (2011)
Fernando Salas – Purchased from Saltillo (Mexican League)
Eduardo Sanchez – Pre-arbitration eligible
Jake Westbrook – 2 years/$17.5M, plus option (2011)

Trade

Octavio Dotel – from TOR w/Marc Rzepczynski, Edwin Jackson and Corey Patterson for Colby Rasmus, Trever Miller, Brian Tallet and P.J. Walters (2011)

David Freese – from SD for Jim Edmonds (2007)

Rafael Furcal – from LAD w/cash considerations and Double-A outfielder Alex Castellanos (2011)

Edwin Jackson – from TOR w/Marc Rzepczynski, Octavio Dotel and Corey Patterson for Colby Rasmus, Trever Miller, Brian Tallet and P.J. Walters (2011)

Corey Patterson – from TOR w/Marc Rzepczynski, Octavio Dotel and Edwin Jackson for Colby Rasmus, Trever Miller, Brian Tallet and P.J. Walters (2011)

Marc Rzepczynski – from TOR w/Octavio Dotel, Edwin Jackson and Corey Patterson for Colby Rasmus, Trever Miller, Brian Tallet and P.J. Walters (2011)

Ryan Theriot – from LAD for Blake Hawksworth (2010)

Adam Wainwright – from ATL w/Jason Marquis and Ray King for J.D. Drew and Eli Marrero (2003)

Date	Opp.	Res.	R	RA	W-L	Date	Opp.	Res.	R	RA	W-L
Thursday, March 31	SD	L	3	5	0-1	Tuesday, May 17	PHI	W	2	1	24-19
Saturday, April 2	SD	L	3	11	0-2	Wednesday, May 18	HOU	W	5	1	25-19
Sunday, April 3	SD	W	2	0	1-2	Thursday, May 19	HOU	W	4	2	26-19
Monday, April 4	PIT	L	3	4	1-3	Friday, May 20	@ KC	L	0	3	26-20
Tuesday, April 5	PIT	W	3	2	2-3	Saturday, May 21	@ KC	W	3	0	27-20
Wednesday, April 6	PIT	L	1	3	2-4	Sunday, May 22	@ KC	W	9	8	28-20
Friday, April 8	@ SF	L	4	5	2-5	Monday, May 23	@ SD	W	3	1	29-20
Saturday, April 9	@ SF	L	2	3	2-6	Tuesday, May 24	@ SD	W	3	2	30-20
Sunday, April 10	@ SF	W	6	1	3-6	Wednesday, May 25	@ SD	L	1	3	30-21
Monday, April 11	@ ARI	W	8	2	4-6	Friday, May 27	@ COL	W	10	3	31-21
Tuesday, April 12	@ ARI	L	8	13	4-7	Saturday, May 28	@ COL	L	4	15	31-22
Wednesday, April 13	@ ARI	W	15	5	5-7	Sunday, May 29	@ COL	W	4	3	32-22
Thursday, April 14	@ LAD	W	9	5	6-7	Monday, May 30	SF	L	3	7	32-23
Friday, April 15	@ LAD	W	11	2	7-7	Tuesday, May 31	SF	W	4	3	33-23
Saturday, April 16	@ LAD	W	9	2	8-7	Wednesday, June 1	SF	L	5	7	33-24
Sunday, April 17	@ LAD	L	1	2	8-8	Thursday, June 2	SF	L	7	12	33-25
Wednesday, April 20	WAS	L	6	8	8-9	Friday, June 3	CHC	W	6	1	34-25
Wednesday, April 20	WAS	W	5	3	9-9	Saturday, June 4	CHC	W	5	4	35-25
Thursday, April 21	WAS	W	5	0	10-9	Sunday, June 5	CHC	W	3	2	36-25
Friday, April 22	CIN	W	4	2	11-9	Tuesday, June 7	@ HOU	W	7	4	37-25
Saturday, April 23	CIN	L	3	5	11-10	Wednesday, June 8	@ HOU	L	1	4	37-26
Sunday, April 24	CIN	W	3	0	12-10	Thursday, June 9	@ HOU	W	9	2	38-26
Tuesday, April 26	@ HOU	L	5	6	12-11	Friday, June 10	@ MIL	L	0	8	38-27
Wednesday, April 27	@ HOU	W	6	5	13-11	Saturday, June 11	@ MIL	L	3	5	38-28
Thursday, April 28	@ HOU	W	11	7	14-11	Sunday, June 12	@ MIL	L	3	4	38-29
Friday, April 29	@ ATL	W	5	3	15-11	Tuesday, June 14	@ WAS	L	6	8	38-30
Saturday, April 30	@ ATL	W	3	2	16-11	Wednesday, June 15	@ WAS	L	0	10	38-31
Sunday, May 1	@ ATL	L	5	6	16-12	Thursday, June 16	@ WAS	L	4	7	38-32
Monday, May 2	FLA	L	5	6	16-13	Friday, June 17	KC	L	4	5	38-33
Tuesday, May 3	FLA	W	7	5	17-13	Saturday, June 18	KC	W	5	4	39-33
Wednesday, May 4	FLA	L	7	8	17-14	Sunday, June 19	KC	W	5	4	40-33
Thursday, May 5	FLA	W	6	3	18-14	Tuesday, June 21	PHI	L	2	10	40-34
Friday, May 6	MIL	W	6	0	19-14	Wednesday, June 22	PHI	L	0	4	40-35
Saturday, May 7	MIL	L	0	4	19-15	Thursday, June 23	PHI	W	12	2	41-35
Sunday, May 8	MIL	W	3	1	20-15	Friday, June 24	TOR	L	4	5	41-36
Tuesday, May 10	@ CHC	W	6	4	21-15	Saturday, June 25	TOR	L	3	6	41-37
Wednesday, May 11	@ CHC	L	4	11	21-16	Sunday, June 26	TOR	L	0	5	41-38
Thursday, May 12	@ CHC	W	9	1	22-16	Tuesday, June 28	@ BAL	W	6	2	42-38
Friday, May 13	@ CIN	L	5	6	22-17	Wednesday, June 29	@ BAL	W	5	1	43-38
Saturday, May 14	@ CIN	L	3	7	22-18	Thursday, June 30	@ BAL	W	9	6	44-38
Sunday, May 15	@ CIN	L	7	9	22-19	Friday, July 1	@ TB	W	5	3	45-38
Monday, May 16	PHI	W	3	1	23-19	Saturday, July 2	@ TB	L	1	5	45-39

REGULAR SEASON RESULTS

Date	Opp.	Res.	R	RA	W-L	Date	Opp.	Res.	R	RA	W-L
Sunday, July 3	@ TB	L	3	8	45-40	Sunday, Aug. 21	@ CHC	W	6	2	67-60
Monday, July 4	CIN	W	1	0	46-40	Monday, Aug. 22	LAD	L	1	2	67-61
Tuesday, July 5	CIN	W	8	1	47-40	Tuesday, Aug. 23	LAD	L	2	13	67-62
Wednesday, July 6	CIN	L	8	9	47-41	Wednesday, Aug. 24	LAD	L	4	9	67-63
Thursday, July 7	ARI	L	1	4	47-42	Thursday, Aug. 25	PIT	W	8	4	68-63
Friday, July 8	ARI	L	6	7	47-43	Friday, Aug. 26	PIT	W	5	4	69-63
Saturday, July 9	ARI	W	7	6	48-43	Saturday, Aug. 27	PIT	L	0	7	69-64
Sunday, July 10	ARI	W	4	2	49-43	Sunday, Aug. 28	PIT	W	7	4	70-64
Friday, July 15	@ CIN	L	5	6	49-44	Tuesday, Aug. 30	@ MIL	W	2	1	71-64
Saturday, July 16	@ CIN	W	4	1	50-44	Wednesday, Aug. 31	@ MIL	W	8	3	72-64
Sunday, July 17	@ CIN	L	1	3	50-45	Thursday, Sept. 1	@ MIL	W	8	4	73-64
Tuesday, July 19	@ NYM	L	2	4	50-46	Friday, Sept. 2	CIN	L	8	11	73-65
Wednesday, July 20	@ NYM	L	5	6	50-47	Saturday, Sept. 3	CIN	W	6	4	74-65
Thursday, July 21	@ NYM	W	6	2	51-47	Sunday, Sept. 4	CIN	L	2	3	74-66
Friday, July 22	@ PIT	W	6	4	52-47	Monday, Sept. 5	MIL	L	1	4	74-67
Saturday, July 23	@ PIT	W	9	1	53-47	Tuesday, Sept. 6	MIL	W	4	2	75-67
Sunday, July 24	@ PIT	L	3	4	53-48	Wednesday, Sept. 7	MIL	W	2	0	76-67
Monday, July 25	HOU	W	10	5	54-48	Friday, Sept. 9	ATL	W	4	3	77-67
Tuesday, July 26	HOU	W	3	1	55-48	Saturday, Sept. 10	ATL	W	4	3	78-67
Wednesday, July 27	HOU	L	2	4	55-49	Sunday, Sept. 11	ATL	W	6	3	79-67
Thursday, July 28	HOU	L	3	5	55-50	Monday, Sept. 12	@ PIT	L	5	6	79-68
Friday, July 29	CHC	W	9	2	56-50	Tuesday, Sept. 13	@ PIT	W	6	4	80-68
Saturday, July 30	CHC	W	13	5	57-50	Wednesday, Sept. 14	@ PIT	W	3	2	81-68
Sunday, July 31	CHC	L	3	6	57-51	Friday, Sept. 16	@ PHI	W	4	2	82-68
Monday, Aug. 1	@ MIL	L	2	6	57-52	Saturday, Sept. 17	@ PHI	L	2	9	82-69
Tuesday, Aug. 2	@ MIL	W	8	7	58-52	Sunday, Sept. 18	@ PHI	W	5	0	83-69
Wednesday, Aug. 3	@ MIL	L	5	10	58-53	Monday, Sept. 19	@ PHI	W	4	3	84-69
Thursday, Aug. 4	@ FLA	W	7	4	59-53	Tuesday, Sept. 20	NYM	W	11	6	85-69
Friday, Aug. 5	@ FLA	W	3	2	60-53	Wednesday, Sept. 21	NYM	W	6	5	86-69
Saturday, Aug. 6	@ FLA	W	2	1	61-53	Thursday, Sept. 22	NYM	L	6	8	86-70
Sunday, Aug. 7	@ FLA	W	8	4	62-53	Friday, Sept. 23	CHC	L	1	5	86-71
Tuesday, Aug. 9	MIL	L	3	5	62-54	Saturday, Sept. 24	CHC	W	2	1	87-71
Wednesday, Aug. 10	MIL	L	1	5	62-55	Sunday, Sept. 25	CHC	W	3	2	88-71
Thursday, Aug. 11	MIL	W	5	2	63-55	Monday, Sept. 26	@ HOU	L	4	5	88-72
Friday, Aug. 12	COL	W	6	1	64-55	Tuesday, Sept. 27	@ HOU	W	13	6	89-72
Saturday, Aug. 13	COL	L	1	6	64-56	Wednesday, Sept. 28	@ HOU	W	8	0	90-72
Sunday, Aug. 14	COL	W	6	2	65-56						
Monday, Aug. 15	@ PIT	L	2	6	65-57						
Tuesday, Aug. 16	@ PIT	L	4	5	65-58						
Wednesday, Aug. 17	@ PIT	W	7	2	66-58						
Friday, Aug. 19	@ CHC	L	4	5	66-59						
Saturday, Aug. 20	@ CHC	L	0	3	66-60						

NO.	PLAYER	B/T	W	L	ERA	SO	BB	SV	BIRTHDATE	BIRTHPLACE
PITCHERS										
41	Mitchell Boggs	R/R	2	3	3.56	48	21	4	2/15/84	Dalton, GA
29	Chris Carpenter	R/R	11	9	3.45	191	55	0	4/27/75	Exeter, NH
28	Octavio Dotel	R/R	5	4	3.50	62	17	3	11/25/73	Santo Domingo, D.R.
54	Jaime Garcia	L/L	13	7	3.56	156	50	0	7/8/86	Reynosa, Mexico
22	Edwin Jackson	R/R	12	9	3.79	148	62	0	9/9/83	Neu-Ulm, West Germany
26	Kyle Lohse	R/R	14	8	3.39	111	42	0	10/4/78	Chico, CA
62	Lance Lynn	R/R	1	1	3.12	40	11	1	5/12/87	Marion County, IN
46	Kyle McClellan	R/R	12	7	4.19	76	43	0	6/12/84	Florissant, MO
30	Jason Motte	R/R	5	2	2.25	63	16	9	6/22/82	Port Huron, MI
53	Arthur Rhodes	L/L	3	4	4.64	21	11	1	10/24/69	Waco, TX
34	Marc Rzepczynski	L/L	2	6	3.34	61	26	0	8/29/85	Yorba Linda, CA
59	Fernando Salas	R/R	5	6	2.28	75	21	24	5/30/85	Huatabampo, Mexico
52	Eduardo Sanchez	R/R	3	1	1.80	35	16	5	2/16/89	Maracay, Venezuela
50	Adam Wainwright	R/R	Did not play due to injury.						8/30/81	Brunswick, GA
35	Jake Westbrook	R/R	12	9	4.66	104	73	0	9/29/77	Athens, GA

NO.	PLAYER	B/T	AB	H	AVG	HR	RBI	OBP	BIRTHDATE	BIRTHPLACE
CATCHERS										
13	Gerald Laird	R/R	95	22	.232	1	12	.302	11/13/79	Westminster, CA
4	Yadier Molina	R/R	475	145	.305	14	65	.349	7/13/82	Bayamon, Puerto Rico
INFIELDERS										
33	Daniel Descalso	L/R	326	86	.264	1	28	.334	10/19/86	Redwood City, CA
23	David Freese	R/R	333	99	.297	10	55	.350	4/28/83	Corpus Christi, TX
15	Rafael Furcal	S/R	333	77	.231	8	28	.298	10/24/77	Loma de Cabrera, D.R.
27	Tyler Greene	R/R	104	22	.212	1	11	.322	8/17/83	Raleigh, NC
5	Albert Pujols	R/R	579	173	.299	37	99	.366	1/16/80	Santo Domingo, D.R.
8	Nick Punto	S/R	133	37	.278	1	20	.388	11/8/77	San Diego, CA
55	Skip Schumaker	L/R	367	104	.283	2	38	.333	2/3/80	Torrance, CA
3	Ryan Theriot	R/R	442	120	.271	1	47	.321	12/7/79	Baton Rouge, LA
OUTFIELDERS										
12	Lance Berkman	S/L	488	147	.301	31	94	.412	2/10/76	Waco, TX
56	Adron Chambers	L/L	8	3	.375	0	4	.375	10/8/86	Pensacola, FL
21	Allen Craig	R/R	200	63	.315	11	40	.362	7/18/84	Mission Viejo, CA
7	Matt Holliday	R/R	446	132	.296	22	75	.388	1/15/80	Stillwater, OK
19	Jon Jay	L/L	455	135	.297	10	37	.344	3/15/85	Miami, FL
44	Corey Patterson	L/R	368	88	.239	6	36	.273	8/13/79	Atlanta, GA

Manager: Tony La Russa (10). Coaches: Dave Duncan (18), Derek Lilliquist (36), Mark McGwire (25), Dave McKay (39), Jose Oquendo (11), Joe Pettini (49).

GAME 1
PHILLIES 11, CARDINALS 6

WHEN LANCE BERKMAN launched a three-run home run off the right-field upper deck in the first inning, the Cardinals officially put the Major Leagues' most successful regular-season team on notice.

After Cardinals starter Kyle Lohse easily shut down the vaunted Phillies early, the Phils got on the board when Shane Victorino knocked in Chase Utley with an RBI single in the fourth.

Just two innings later, the Phillies struck again. With two men on, Ryan Howard won a long battle with Lohse in a loud way, slamming a three-run homer to give Philadelphia a 4-3 lead.

The Phils were not done, though. In the midst of all the excitement from the Howard homer, Raul Ibanez sent the Philadelphia crowd into a frenzy with a two-run jolt, which proved to be more than enough support for Roy Halladay, who recovered from his early struggles to retire 21 straight Cardinals hitters en route to the 11-6 win.

	1	2	3	4	5	6	7	8	9	R	H	E
ST. LOUIS	3	0	0	0	0	0	0	0	3	6	7	1
PHILADELPHIA	0	0	0	1	0	5	3	2	x	11	14	0

WP: Halladay LP: Lohse
HR: STL: Berkman; PHI: Howard, Ibanez

After a year's hiatus, the Cardinals were once again introduced before a playoff contest — Game 1 of the NLDS at Philadelphia's Citizens Bank Park.

Lance Berkman followed a resurgent regular season by belting a three-run shot off the Phillies' Roy Halladay in the opening stanza of Game 1.

GAME 2
CARDINALS 5, PHILLIES 4

AFTER COMING BACK from a 10.5-game deficit in the Wild Card race to make the playoffs, the Cardinals proved that they could handle adversity.

That is what they faced after their ace right-hander, Chris Carpenter, struggled on three days' rest in Game 2, spotting Philadelphia a four-run lead after just two innings with Cliff Lee on the mound for the Phillies. Just like in September, though, the Cardinals did not fold. They rallied for 12 hits off Lee — surpassing his high of 11 in the regular season — inducing the most damage in a three-run fourth inning that cut the lead to one.

With a dominant performance from its bullpen, the St. Louis club continued to pressure Philadelphia, tying the game in the sixth inning on a Jon Jay single that scored Ryan Theriot.

The Cardinals finally pulled ahead in the seventh, scoring their fifth run off Lee when Allen Craig led off with a triple and Albert Pujols singled him home, getting the win and evening up the series at a game apiece.

	1	2	3	4	5	6	7	8	9	R	H	E
ST. LOUIS	0	0	0	3	0	1	1	0	0	5	13	0
PHILADELPHIA	3	1	0	0	0	0	0	0	0	4	6	0

WP: Dotel LP: Lee SV: Motte
HR: None

Cardinals center fielder Jon Jay got tagged out at home in the fourth inning, but with two RBI and a St. Louis victory on the night, he laughed last.

The light-hitting Ryan Theriot recorded two doubles, two runs and an RBI on the night to help the Cardinals even the NLDS at one win apiece.

"WELL, I MEAN, WE WERE NOT HAPPY BECAUSE WE KNOW WHO LEE IS, HOW HE PITCHES, THE TEAM HE PITCHES IN FRONT OF. BUT WE KEEP THINGS REAL SIMPLE. WE ARE JUST GOING TO PLAY NINE, COME HELL OR HIGH WATER."
—Cardinals Manager Tony La Russa on falling behind, 4-0

GAME 3
PHILLIES 3, CARDINALS 2

WITH JAIME GARCIA and Cole Hamels dealing, runs were difficult to come by in Game 3. Hamels fought through control problems to strike out eight and put zeroes on the board in each of his six innings of work.

Garcia cruised along through most of the game, as well. He retired the Phillies in order in four of the first five innings, facing much less drama than his counterpart with the Phillies, which made it all the more surprising that Garcia flinched first.

With a 0-0 tie in the top of the seventh, Phillies Manager Charlie Manuel called on Ben Francisco to pinch-hit with two men on and two outs. Francisco delivered, homering into the Phillies' bullpen and giving his team a 3-0 lead.

But the Cards would not go down without a fight. After scoring a run in the seventh, they loaded the bases with one out for Allen Craig in the eighth. Manuel didn't panic, though, instead calling on closer Ryan Madson to put out the fire. Madson responded by inducing an inning-ending double play to help the Phillies hold on for a 3-2 win.

	1	2	3	4	5	6	7	8	9	R	H	E
PHILADELPHIA	0	0	0	0	0	0	3	0	0	3	7	0
ST. LOUIS	0	0	0	0	0	0	1	0	1	2	12	0

WP: Hamels LP: Garcia SV: Madson
HR: PHI: Francisco

Ben Francisco emerged as an unexpected hero for the Phillies in Game 3, coming off the bench to break the scoreless tie with a three-run blast.

In a pitchers' duel, someone has to be the hard-luck loser; unfortunately for St. Louis, Jaime Garcia — who went unscathed through six innings — was it.

GAME 4
CARDINALS 5, PHILLIES 3

WHEN PHILADELPHIA SCORED two runs before the Cardinals could record an out in the first, St. Louis's chances to extend the series looked slim. But starting pitcher Edwin Jackson settled down and kept the Phillies at bay, holding them to just the two runs in six innings and giving his team a chance to get back into the game.

Lance Berkman immediately responded with an RBI double that scored Skip Schumaker in the bottom of the first. And in the fourth, David Freese, beginning what would be a stellar postseason run, helped the Cardinals fight back. Down, 2-1, in the fourth, Freese delivered a two-run double to give St. Louis the lead. Then, in the sixth inning, he came through with a crushing two-run homer to give the Cards a seemingly insurmountable three-run lead with just three innings to go.

The St. Louis bullpen, which stepped up in the play-offs after an up-and-down regular season, never gave the Phillies a chance to get back into the game and held on for a 5-3 win, sending the series to a decisive Game 5.

	1	2	3	4	5	6	7	8	9	R	H	E
PHILADELPHIA	2	0	0	0	0	0	0	1	0	3	7	1
ST. LOUIS	1	0	0	2	0	2	0	0	x	5	6	0

WP: Jackson LP: Oswalt SV: Motte
HR: STL: Freese

David Freese (center) gave the Cardinals' bullpen some breathing room with a two-run shot in the sixth, part of a four-RBI night for the third baseman.

Edwin Jackson recovered from a two-run first inning to shut down the Phillies in the next five, allowing the Cardinals to come back and tie the series.

GAME 5
CARDINALS 1, PHILLIES 0

THE MANTRA GOING into Game 5 was to get to him early — "him" referring to Phillies ace Roy Halladay. The Cardinals didn't get much, with Halladay escaping the first having allowed just one run after Rafael Furcal and Skip Schumaker started the game with a triple and a double, but it proved to be plenty for Chris Carpenter.

The big right-hander, who struggled in Game 2 in Philadelphia, returned to quiet the Phillies faithful, going toe-to-toe with Doc and refusing to give an inch. He shut down the Phillies all night and made sure that the Cardinals' first-inning run held up. Even though Halladay rebounded to keep the Cardinals off the board for the rest of the night, it didn't matter, as Carpenter dominated.

All told, Carpenter scattered three hits and five base runners, shutting out the 102-win Phillies and sending the Cardinals to the NLCS for the first time since 2006.

	1	2	3	4	5	6	7	8	9	R	H	E
ST. LOUIS	1	0	0	0	0	0	0	0	0	1	6	1
PHILADELPHIA	0	0	0	0	0	0	0	0	0	0	3	2

WP: Carpenter LP: Halladay
HR: None

Clockwise from bottom left: Nick Punto tagged Chase Utley out on a steal attempt; Rafael Furcal tripled to lead off the game; the Cardinals celebrated.

GAME 5
CARDINALS 1, PHILLIES 0

The Cardinals reveled in their Game 5 victory with a champagne shower in the clubhouse.

NO ROOM FOR ERROR

GOING UP AGAINST Roy Halladay in a winner-take-all postseason game is something every fan fears — and every competitor relishes. Cardinals ace Chris Carpenter — he of the 2005 NL Cy Young Award, a 2006 World Series ring, and a 3.38 ERA and 5-2 record in 10 career postseason starts heading into the game — certainly thrived in Game 5 of the NLDS against Doc and the heavily-favored Phillies. He practically willed his team to victory with a three-hit, zero-walk shutout. In doing so, he became just the third pitcher ever to throw a complete-game victory in a 1-0, winner-take-all postseason game. The New York Yankees' Ralph Terry accomplished the feat when he shut out the Giants in Game 7 of the 1962 World Series, as did the Twins' Jack Morris with a 10-inning gem in Game 7 of the 1991 Fall Classic against the Braves.

GAME 1
BREWERS 9, CARDINALS 6

WITH TWO OF the best offenses in the Senior Circuit facing off in the NLCS, fans could expect plenty of fireworks. Both the Cardinals and Brewers delivered in that regard from the series' opening stanza.

The Cards got on the board in the top of the first inning thanks to a Matt Holliday RBI single off Zack Greinke. That deficit was quickly erased in the bottom half of the frame when Milwaukee outfielder Ryan Braun smoked a ball to deep left-center field for a two-run homer. Cardinals third baseman David Freese would begin to build his case for the NLCS MVP Award by putting his team back in front with a three-run shot in the fourth inning. But again, Braun, coupled with fellow Brewers masher Prince Fielder, would bring Milwaukee back with a two-run double and a two-run homer, respectively, in the bottom of the fifth.

Another two runs that inning from a Yuniesky Betancourt homer would put the Brewers up, 8-5, a lead they would not relinquish as they went on to win, 9-6.

	1	2	3	4	5	6	7	8	9	R	H	E
ST. LOUIS	1	0	0	3	1	0	1	0	0	6	9	1
MILWAUKEE	2	0	0	0	6	0	1	0	x	9	11	0

WP: Greinke **LP:** Garcia **SV:** Axford
HR: STL: Freese; **MIL:** Betancourt, Braun, Fielder

Rickie Weeks (left) and Prince Fielder were pumped up after Fielder launched a two-run homer that put the Brewers ahead for good in Game 1.

The normally reliable Jaime Garcia settled down after a tough first inning, but then came unraveled in the fifth, allowing six total runs in the game.

GAME 1
BREWERS 9, CARDINALS 6

David Freese continued to swing a hot bat in the NLCS, briefly putting the Cardinals ahead in Game 1 with a three-run homer in the fourth inning.

GAME 2
CARDINALS 12, BREWERS 3

NOT FAZED BY blowing a three-run lead in Game 1, the Cardinals jumped on Brewers pitching in the first inning, scoring two runs on a homer from Albert Pujols. This would be just a precursor to the slugfest that the team — and Pujols, who would go 4 for 5 with five RBI — enjoyed the rest of the game. David Freese hit his second home run of the series as five players, including Nick Punto and Yadier Molina, recorded multi-hit games for St. Louis.

Meanwhile, the Cardinals' Edwin Jackson cruised through the first three innings, highlighted by a 1-2-3 third in which he struck out the side. It's hard to keep a good offense down for long, though, and the Brewers managed to get two runs on the board in the bottom of the fourth to cut the deficit to 5-2. But that would be as close as they got the rest of the way as the Cardinals put up seven more runs en route to a 12-3 win.

	1	2	3	4	5	6	7	8	9	R	H	E
ST. LOUIS	2	0	2	1	2	0	4	0	1	12	17	0
MILWAUKEE	0	0	0	2	0	0	0	1	0	3	8	1

WP: Lynn **LP:** Marcum
HR: STL: Freese, Pujols; MIL: Fielder, Weeks

For a second straight game, David Freese (top) helped St. Louis with his bat, collecting two RBI, and Albert Pujols scored on a wild pitch in the fith inning.

ALL IN THE FAMILY

CARDINALS CATCHER YADIER Molina was just 20 years old and still two seasons away from making his Major League debut when his older brothers, Bengie (then 28) and Jose (27) won World Series rings as members of the Anaheim Angels in 2002. But nearly a decade later, Yadier has started to establish himself as the cream of the Molina crop.

With three Gold Glove Awards on his resume and a third straight All-Star Game appearance in 2011, Yadier has already acquired more accolades than both of his brothers combined. This season, the emotional leader of the Cardinals became the first of the three brothers to finish with an OPS better than .800, as he set career highs in home runs (14), doubles (32) and batting average (.305). Now a two-time champ, the 29-year-old Yadier sits at the kids' table no more.

Albert Pujols went berserk in St. Louis's Game 2 win, going 4 for 5 with three doubles and five RBI.

GAME 2
CARDINALS 12, BREWERS 3

A part-time player during his first season with the Cardinals, Nick Punto contributed to the Game 2 onslaught with two hits and two runs batted in.

"WHEN I HAVE THE BIG BOYS BEHIND ME, MY JOB IS SIMPLE: JUST GET ON BASE. I WAS ABLE TO DO THAT TODAY. IF I CAN GET ON BASE, IT GIVES THEM THE OPPORTUNITY TO DO WHAT THEY DO, WHICH IS DRIVE IN RUNS. IT ALL KIND OF WORKED OUT FOR US TODAY." —Cardinals outfielder Jon Jay

GAME 3
CARDINALS 4, BREWERS 3

FOR A THIRD consecutive game, the Cardinals jumped all over Brewers pitching in the first inning, scoring four times in the bottom of the frame off Milwaukee's ace right-hander Yovani Gallardo. The first five batters reached base for St. Louis, highlighted by back-to-back run-scoring doubles from outfielder Jon Jay and first baseman Albert Pujols. David Freese added an RBI double of his own a few batters later.

Not getting down on themselves despite the early 4-0 deficit, the Brewers began to claw back in the top of the second with an RBI single from Yuniesky Betancourt and a sac fly off the bat of Gallardo. With another run in the third inning thanks to a Mark Kotsay homer, the Brewers were back in business, but that would be all that Cardinals ace Chris Carpenter would allow.

The four runs St. Louis scored in the first held up, as the bullpen — anchored by closer Jason Motte and his three strikeouts to four batters — didn't allow a hit in the final four innings of a 4-3 win that gave the Cardinals a 2-games-to-1 advantage.

	1	2	3	4	5	6	7	8	9	R	H	E
MILWAUKEE	0	2	1	0	0	0	0	0	0	3	6	0
ST. LOUIS	4	0	0	0	0	0	0	0	x	4	9	0

WP: Carpenter LP: Gallardo SV: Motte HR: MIL: Kotsay

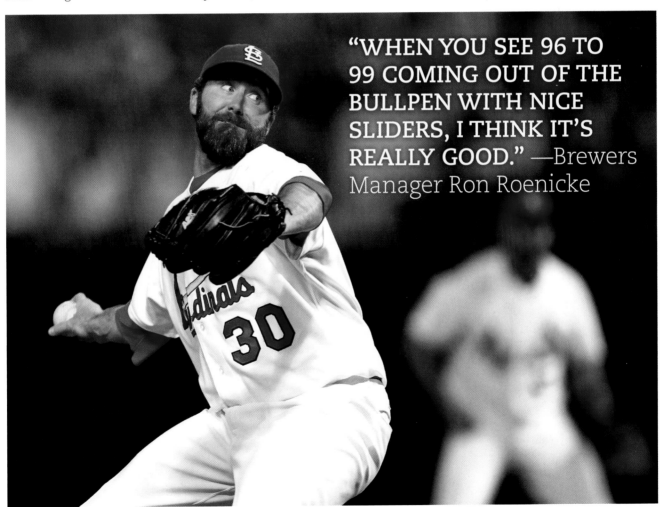

"WHEN YOU SEE 96 TO 99 COMING OUT OF THE BULLPEN WITH NICE SLIDERS, I THINK IT'S REALLY GOOD." —Brewers Manager Ron Roenicke

He didn't start closing games until late August, but Jason Motte was lights-out in that role during the NLCS, not allowing a base runner in 4.2 innings.

GAME 3
CARDINALS 4, BREWERS 3

Chris Carpenter didn't have his A game, but he kept the Brewers' powerful lineup in check enough to hold on for the win.

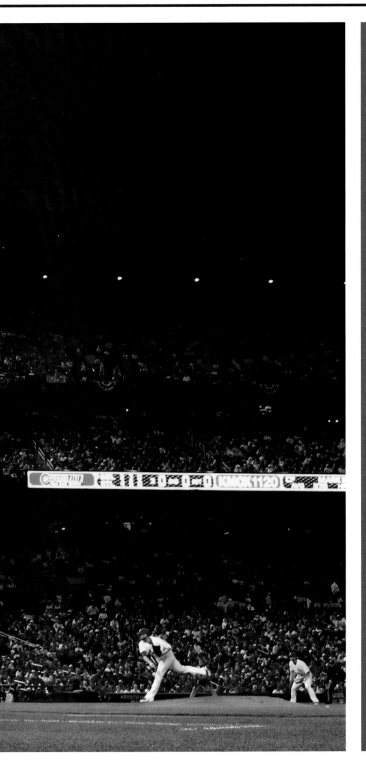

WHAT A RELIEF

Fernando Salas

IF DURING THE 2011 All-Star break you had asked the Cardinals which area of their team most needed improvement, the bullpen would have been a common response. St. Louis's relief pitching during the first half of the season left much to be desired, as the bullpen recorded a 4.00 ERA, a 1.33 WHIP and just a 2.25 strikeout-to-walk ratio. But that's one of the great things about a 162-game season; it leaves plenty of time to turn things around.

Using a multitude of combinations and closers — including Fernando Salas and Jason Motte — to finish out games, Manager Tony La Russa saw a drastic improvement in his 'pen after the All-Star break, as it posted a 3.38 second-half ERA with a 1.19 WHIP and a 2.82 K/BB ratio. The bullpen proved just as much a reason as any for the team's late playoff push and successful run through the postseason.

GAME 4
BREWERS 4, CARDINALS 2

ALTHOUGH THE CARDINALS again jumped ahead early in Game 4 with a Matt Holliday solo shot in the second and an Allen Craig home run in the third, the Brewers' No. 4 starter — left-hander Randy Wolf — would limit the damage and help keep the Brewers out of a 3-games-to-1 hole. Wolf struck out six in seven innings of work as the Brewers' offense came to life in the fourth inning with an RBI double from Jerry Hairston followed by a run-scoring single from Yuniesky Betancourt.

Ryan Braun continued his stellar postseason performance by putting Milwaukee up, 3-2, with an RBI single in the fifth, and the Brewers added another run in the sixth on an RBI by backup catcher George Kottaras. Brewers closer John Axford recorded a scoreless ninth inning for the save, knotting the series at two games apiece.

	1	2	3	4	5	6	7	8	9	R	H	E
MILWAUKEE	0	0	0	2	1	1	0	0	0	4	10	1
ST. LOUIS	0	1	1	0	0	0	0	0	0	2	8	1

WP: Wolf **LP:** Lohse **SV:** Axford
HR: STL: Craig, Holliday

Ryan Braun, who would record a .968 OPS in the NLCS, helped the Brewers even the series with a go-ahead RBI single in the fifth inning.

Matt Holliday's second-inning solo home run — his sole longball of the League Championship Series — put the Cardinals on the board first in Game 4.

"IT'S TWO REALLY TOUGH TEAMS. THERE'S NO WAY I COULD PUT INTO WORDS THE INTENSITY THAT'S THERE EVERY INNING. YOU KNOW HOW IMPORTANT EVERY OUT IS. YOU KNOW HOW GOOD EITHER TEAM, IF THEY HAVE AN OPPORTUNITY TO SCORE, IS AT TAKING ADVANTAGE OF THAT OPPORTUNITY."
—Brewers pitcher Randy Wolf

GAME 5
CARDINALS 7, BREWERS 1

AN ALREADY SLOPPY postseason for Brewers fielders turned nightmarish in Game 5. With St. Louis leading, 1-0, in the bottom of the second thanks to a Yadier Molina double, the Cardinals had a man on second and third with two outs and starting pitcher Jaime Garcia at the plate.

The left-handed Garcia hit a routine groundball to third baseman Jerry Hairston, who let it go between his legs for a two-run error. This would be the first of four Milwaukee errors, and the Cardinals took advantage of another miscue in the sixth when Yuniesky Betancourt let a grounder ricochet off the heel of his glove with two outs. The following batter, Albert Pujols, hit a single to left to score another run and chase Brewers starting pitcher Zack Greinke from the game. Matt Holliday added two more runs in the eighth with an RBI double to give his team a comfortable 7-1 cushion that would hold up.

	1	2	3	4	5	6	7	8	9	R	H	E
MILWAUKEE	0	0	0	0	1	0	0	0	0	1	9	4
ST. LOUIS	0	3	0	1	0	1	0	2	x	7	10	0

WP: Dotel LP: Greinke SV: Motte HR: None

With Manager Tony La Russa ready to use his full allotment of relievers, Jaime Garcia pitched just 4.2 innings, but held the Brewers to one run.

"JUST LUCKY AGAINST BRAUN, THAT'S WHAT I CAN SAY. I TRY TO MAKE MY PITCHES EVERY TIME I SEE HIM. I GUESS I'M LUCKY AGAINST HIM, AND I WOULD LOVE TO BE THE SAME WHEN THE SERIES IS OVER." —Cardinals pitcher Octavio Dotel

Octavio Dotel came up huge out of the bullpen throughout the NLCS, including 1.1 shutout innings with two strikeouts in Game 5.

GAME 5
CARDINALS 7, BREWERS 1

Yadier Molina broke a scoreless tie early in Game 5, smoking an opposite-field double to plate Lance Berkman in the second inning.

With a 7-1 Game 5 victory in the books, the Cardinals left their home ballpark knowing they would just need a split in Milwaukee to win the pennant.

GAME 6
CARDINALS 12, BREWERS 6

LIKE THEY DID in Game 2, the Cardinals jumped all over Brewers starting pitcher Shaun Marcum right out of the gate, scoring four first-inning runs on an RBI single from Lance Berkman and a three-run shot from David Freese. After Milwaukee's Corey Hart shaved one run off the deficit in the bottom half of the inning with a home run off Edwin Jackson, Rafael Furcal launched a solo shot of his own in the second.

Down, 5-1, the Brewers fought back with two more home runs in the bottom of the second to cut the score to 5-4, and the shootout was officially on. Albert Pujols hit the sixth home run of the game in a four-run third inning for St. Louis.

In the bottom of the seventh, with the Cardinals up, 11-6, reliever Octavio Dotel got Ryan Braun out on strikes, the third time he struck out the Brewers' star in the series and ninth time in 11 at-bats against him in his career.

The Cards went on to win, 12-6, as Freese won NLCS MVP honors with three homers and a 1.691 OPS.

	1	2	3	4	5	6	7	8	9	R	H	E
ST. LOUIS	4	1	4	0	2	0	0	1	0	12	14	0
MILWAUKEE	1	3	0	1	1	0	0	0	0	6	7	3

WP: Rzepczynski **LP:** Marcum
HR: STL: Freese, Furcal, Pujols; MIL: Hart, Lucroy, Weeks

Three was the magic number for David Freese in the clinching game, as he collected three hits, scored three times and drove in three runs.

Rafael Furcal, who has averaged just nine home runs a season in his 12-year career, flexed his muscles in the second inning with a solo home run.

"WE BELIEVE. I THINK THAT'S WHAT YOU'VE GOT TO DO IN THIS GAME. WE'VE GOT A GROUP OF GUYS WITH SOME TALENT, DESIRE AND JUST A TON OF HEART. COMING BACK FROM 10-AND-A-HALF GAMES, OBVIOUSLY IT'S A TOUGH BATTLE. BUT WE KEPT PLUGGING; WE KEPT PUSHING. IT'S KIND OF SURREAL THAT WE'RE HERE, BUT THIS TEAM DESERVES WHAT IT HAS BEEN REWARDED."
—Cardinals third baseman David Freese

GAME 6
CARDINALS 12, BREWERS 6

Clockwise from left: Jason Motte, Daniel Descalso and Yadier Molina led the celebratory mosh pit following the Cardinals' pennant-clinching victory.

With the Cardinals up, 6-4, in the top of the third inning, Matt Holliday extended the lead when he scored on a sacrifice fly by Nick Punto.

MAXIMUM OVERDRIVE

TIME AND AGAIN, the postseason has proven to be a stage where heroes emerge from the unlikeliest of places. For the 2011 Cardinals, of course there were the usual suspects, such as Matt Holliday, Albert Pujols and Chris Carpenter, each of whom excelled in the pressure cooker of October baseball. But their playoff contributions likely would have gone for naught had it not been for the performance of 28-year-old third baseman David Freese.

In 184 career regular-season games, Freese has put up decent numbers, hitting .298 with 15 homers, a .354 OBP and a .783 OPS. In the first two rounds of the playoffs alone, though, he hit four home runs with a 1.315 OPS. His first big blast came in Game 4 of the NLDS as he helped even the series with the Phillies at two games apiece on the strength of a two-run homer. He reached Pujols levels once the NLCS came around, slugging three more home runs and getting on base at a .600 clip to earn series MVP honors.

GAME 1
CARDINALS 3, RANGERS 2

IF THE EARLY chapters of the 2011 postseason story taught fans anything, it was to expect nail-biters. Amidst a sea of red at Busch Stadium, the Cardinals edged the powerful Rangers in a pitchers' duel, 3-2, to jump out to an early Series lead. Starting pitcher Chris Carpenter set the tone, not only by bringing his typically overpowering stuff, but also by diving for a throw from Albert Pujols while covering first base in the top of the opening frame to get the out. Belly-to-the-ground, Carpenter slid across

	1	2	3	4	5	6	7	8	9	R	H	E
TEXAS	0	0	0	0	2	0	0	0	0	2	6	0
ST. LOUIS	0	0	0	2	0	1	0	0	x	3	6	0

WP: Carpenter **LP:** Wilson **SV:** Motte
HR: TEX: Napoli

the bag to retire Elvis Andrus for the second out of the inning. "That Carp play was scary, but I didn't have a lot of time," said Pujols. "He got his arm in there and thank God he was okay."

After Carpenter and Texas starter C.J. Wilson traded zeroes for three-and-a-half innings in chilly St. Louis — the game time temperature was 49 degrees, the third-lowest ever for a World Series Game 1, and it continued to drop as the night wore on — the Redbirds got on the board first with a two-run single down the first-base line by Lance Berkman. The Rangers struck back with a two-run homer by Mike Napoli in the fifth, then pinch-hitter Allen Craig laced an RBI single off Alexi Ogando in the sixth for what turned out to be the night's decisive blow.

In addition to putting Craig in the perfect situation coming off the bench, Manager Tony La Russa also made a slew of pitching moves that worked out perfectly for his club. The five St. Louis relievers combined to toss three shutout innings, permitting just two base runners in the process. Jason Motte, the only 'pen mate to pitch a full inning in Game 1, shut the door with a perfect ninth. "Tony makes all the right moves," said reliever Mark Rzepczynski, who struck out the two hitters he faced in the seventh inning. "Over and over again, Tony puts the right guys on the mound and at the plate."

With the victory, the Cardinals surpassed the Giants and Dodgers to claim second place on the all-time World Series games played list with 106. (The Yankees head the list with 225.) More importantly, they gained an early one-game lead, but they knew they were far from done. "I don't believe in momentum," Pujols said. "We play this game every day to win and we need to come back and do that again tomorrow. Turn the page."

Lance Berkman singled down the right-field line in the fourth inning to score Albert Pujols and Matt Holliday, accounting for the first runs of the Fall Classic.

"I WENT TO A FEW CARDINALS PLAYOFF GAMES WHEN I WAS GROWING UP. WE SEE THE PICTURES AROUND THIS BALLPARK OF THOSE GREAT PAST WORLD SERIES TEAMS AND WANT THAT TO BE US. WE WANT TO BE THE GUYS ON THE WALL." —Cardinals third baseman David Freese

Jason Motte (left) got the save in Game 1, but the whole 'pen deserved credit; Michelle Obama championed the Welcome Back Veterans cause at the game.

GAME 1
CARDINALS 3, RANGERS 2

DOWN AND DIRTY

MANAGERS NEVER WANT to see their No. 1 starting pitcher hit the dirt, but in the case of Chris Carpenter, Tony La Russa may not mind. Carpenter, a 6-foot-6 right-hander, became the Cardinals' emotional leader down the stretch run, and that continued through October. Sprinting to cover first base on a roller to Albert Pujols in the top of the first in Game 1, Carpenter set off on a foot race with Rangers No. 2 hitter Elvis Andrus and dove for Pujols' throw, then slid across the bag to beat the speedy runner. It can't be pretty to see the ace of your staff flat on the ground, but La Russa found humor in the situation since it turned out so well. "The only thing I kidded him about was if he should have put his face in front of [Andrus's] spike," La Russa said. "Then he could have been bleeding for the rest of the game and he could have been another Curt Schilling. That would have been a hell of a sight, because he has always talked about how hockey players get gashed and they're still out there playing, but baseball players get taken out."

The lay-it-on-the-line style became a staple of Carpenter's approach this fall. He started things off with a dramatic complete-game shutout against Houston on the final day of the regular season to send St. Louis to the play-offs. He then shut out the mighty Phillies in the winner-take-all Game 5 of the Division Series. His opponent in that 1-0 duel was none other than the defending NL Cy Young Award winner, his former teammate and close friend Roy Halladay. Carpenter's next turn came in Game 1 of the Fall Classic. "He's our leader out there," said Allen Craig, "and to have him out there on the mound for Game 1 worked out perfectly."

Carp worked six innings, allowing just two runs for the win to push his career playoff record to 8-2, surpassing Bob Gibson for the Cardinals' post-season wins record and ranking first among active Major League starters.

Allen Craig's pinch-hit single with two outs in the sixth (near right) was just out of the reach of Rangers right fielder Nelson Cruz (far right), allowing the go-ahead run to score. Carpenter set the tone for a tough win in Game 1 when he made a diving play in the first inning to beat Elvis Andrus to the bag.

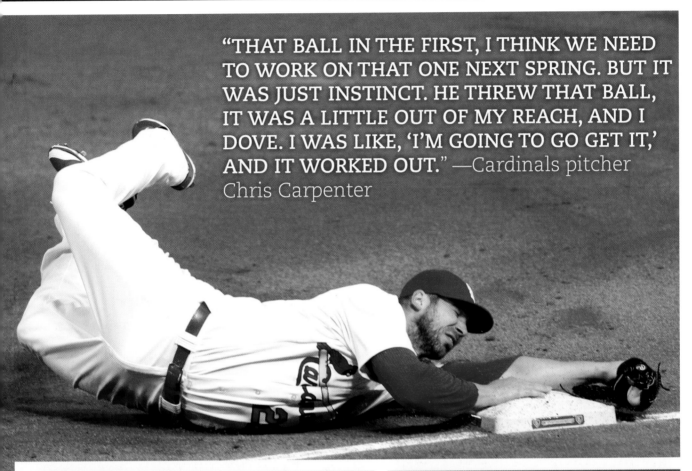

"THAT BALL IN THE FIRST, I THINK WE NEED TO WORK ON THAT ONE NEXT SPRING. BUT IT WAS JUST INSTINCT. HE THREW THAT BALL, IT WAS A LITTLE OUT OF MY REACH, AND I DOVE. I WAS LIKE, 'I'M GOING TO GO GET IT,' AND IT WORKED OUT." —Cardinals pitcher Chris Carpenter

GAME 2
RANGERS 2, CARDINALS 1

THE 2011 WORLD Series was supposed to be contested between two great lineups and two extremely solid bullpens, with relievers summoned at any point in the game.

What it wasn't supposed to be — what no one could reasonably have expected — was a setting for a pitching duel between Texas's Colby Lewis and the Cardinals' Jaime Garcia.

With due respect to the two pitchers, Game 2 — once the aces' starts were out of the way in Game 1 — was supposed to be the first real demonstration of Tony La Russa's and Ron Washington's famously itchy trigger

	1	2	3	4	5	6	7	8	9	R	H	E
TEXAS	0	0	0	0	0	0	0	0	2	2	5	1
ST. LOUIS	0	0	0	0	0	0	1	0	0	1	6	1

WP: Adams LP: Motte SV: Feliz
HR: None

fingers. But both starters pitched into the seventh inning, and entering the ninth, the Cardinals were ahead, 1-0, three outs from flying to Texas on the wings of a two-game World Series cushion.

In that final frame, though, the Rangers' offense finally struck against closer Jason Motte: a single and a stolen base by Ian Kinsler; an Elvis Andrus hit that moved the tying run to third (and a rare misplay by Albert Pujols that allowed Andrus to take second); and, finally, consecutive sacrifice flies, the first tying the game, the second putting the Rangers ahead. From there, it was time for dominant closer Neftali Feliz to do as Neftali Feliz does. Rangers win, 2-1. Series tied, one game apiece. Quite a turnaround. "It's a huge difference," reliever Mike Adams said. "If it's 0-2, our backs are really up against the wall. For us to pull that out in the top of the ninth like that, that's huge."

Of course, for all the deserved kudos Lewis received in the victors' clubhouse, the outcome might have been totally different but for some incredible defense by Andrus. In the fourth and fifth innings, Andrus made tremendous plays going to his left; the first one starting a double play (credit also to Kinsler, who received the backhand flip with his bare hand and made an incredible turn), the second one a remarkable dive to snare a ball up the middle and a glove flip that perfectly led Kinsler to the bag.

The latter play saved at least one run, and with offense scarce in Game 2, it's impossible to overstate the impact of both plays. "Elvis has been making those plays all year long," Lewis said. "It was outstanding. I'm a pretty even-keeled guy, and I gave it a fist-pump. It definitely saved a run."

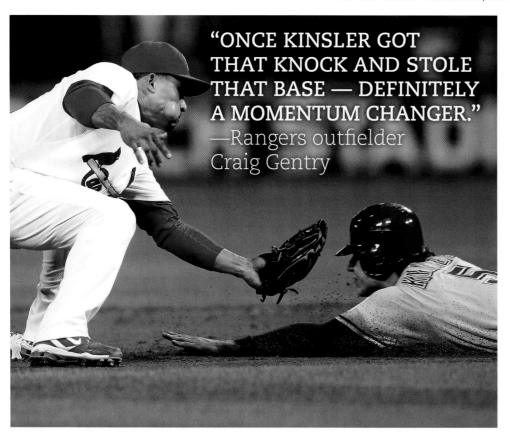

"ONCE KINSLER GOT THAT KNOCK AND STOLE THAT BASE — DEFINITELY A MOMENTUM CHANGER."
—Rangers outfielder Craig Gentry

Ian Kinsler narrowly slid in safely under Rafael Furcal's tag to steal second base in the ninth inning.

Elvis Andrus and Ian Kinsler teamed up for some spectacular defense in Game 2, including a dive-and-flip play to get Jaime Garcia at second base.

GAME 2
RANGERS 2, CARDINALS 1

"BOTH TEAMS ARE PITCHING VERY WELL. AS FAR AS OFFENSE GOES, IT'S NOT LIKE YOU CAN BRING THE STICKS EVERY NIGHT."
—Cardinals outfielder Allen Craig

David Freese (left) scored the Cardinals' lone run, while Jaime Garcia threw seven shutout innings to keep St. Louis ahead for much of the game.

COMING UP CLUTCH

TONY LA RUSSA has been labeled a genius by fans of his in-game decisions. But he'll be the first to admit that players who execute deserve the credit. Allen Craig is one of those. Stepping into a clutch off-the-bench role this October with one pinch-hit in Game 3 of the NLCS, Craig was just getting warmed up for the World Series stage.

With the score knotted at two in the sixth inning of Game 1, Craig delivered a pinch-hit single off Rangers reliever Alexi Ogando that drove in the eventual winning run in the Cardinals' 3-2 victory. "It was cold and a little tough to warm up off the bench, but you can't let the cold bother you at the World Series," Craig said after Game 1. "I had my legs loose and I was looking for an opportunity."

Opportunity presented itself in Game 2, in an almost identical situation. La Russa once more turned to Craig with two outs and two on. Craig laced another RBI single — again off Ogando — to give the Rangers a 1-0 lead. "I just try to keep it simple when I'm pinch-hitting," Craig said. "You can't miss the pitches that are out over the plate, and I've been able to get the barrel on them." His team wouldn't hold on for the win this time, but that didn't diminish the ability to perform under pressure that Craig displayed. "He's a good weapon," said La Russa.

GAME 3
CARDINALS 16, RANGERS 7

IT'S HARD TO believe in retrospect, but before Game 3 of the 2011 Fall Classic turned into the Albert Pujols show, fans at Rangers Ballpark had already seen a thrilling first few innings that featured the Cardinals seeming to pull away, only to have Texas answer right back. There's certainly some irony in the fact that the very circumstance that made the game so lopsided and anti-climactic — Pujols' procession of longballs — is the same thing that fans will hold on to forever.

"Incredible to watch," said Cardinals starter Kyle Lohse, who couldn't record an out in the fourth inning, and subsequently left the game but was backed by a titanic

	1	2	3	4	5	6	7	8	9	R	H	E
ST. LOUIS	1	0	0	4	3	4	2	1	1	16	15	0
TEXAS	0	0	0	3	3	0	1	0	0	7	13	3

WP: Lynn LP: Harrison
HR: STL: Craig, Pujols 3
TEX: Young, Cruz

offensive effort. "One of those games that you're going to be telling your kids about."

In the end, 23 runs had scored, and the Cardinals had more than doubled up their hosts, winning 16-7. And while "Albert Pujols, Albert Pujols, Albert Pujols, Albert Pujols" might be a fitting recap for the game, there were plenty of highlights from the rest of the Redbirds' cast.

Matt Holliday, for one, spent the game's first half in the spotlight. In the fourth inning, when the Cardinals held a 1-0 advantage, the St. Louis left fielder was the beneficiary of a missed call at first base, as he was ruled safe despite having been tagged before he reached the bag. The Cardinals would plate four runs in the inning, and while the Rangers hung around until the sixth, it's impossible to know the impact that second life had on St. Louis's offense.

But there's no doubting the impact that Holliday's other highlight had on the game. In the bottom of the frame, the Rangers had runners at the corners with one out and three runs home already. Ian Kinsler lofted a ball to left, which Holliday fielded easily as Mike Napoli tagged from third. Holliday's cannon was perfectly targeted, and catcher Yadier Molina planted the tag on Napoli to end the threat and suck the air out of Rangers Ballpark.

"Amazing," Molina said. "I think that was a big momentum changer. I think it was a huge moment."

"You never know how many runs it's going to take, especially in this park, to beat those guys," added Holliday. "So any run you could save is good."

The teams combined for 28 hits as neither starting pitcher made it out of the fourth inning. The clubs left 38 men on base over the course of the four-plus hours. And, oh yeah, Prince Albert hit three home runs, just the fourth time that has happened in World Series history. It might not have been Shakespeare, but it was still a night full of drama.

Albert Pujols got a hit off five of the six pitchers who appeared for Texas and added six RBI to put the Cardinals past the Rangers and take a 2-games-to-1 Series advantage.

Albert Pujols owned the night in Game 3 with a trio of mammoth longballs. Fans and players in Rangers Ballpark looked on as he let one soar.

"HO-HUM. I EXPECTED PUJOLS TO HIT IT, I REALLY DID. HE'S THE GREATEST HITTER, IN MY OPINION, EVER. SO IT'S NOT SURPRISING THAT HE WOULD HAVE THE GREATEST PERFORMANCE IN WORLD SERIES HISTORY." —Cardinals outfielder Lance Berkman

GAME 3
CARDINALS 16, RANGERS 7

Overshadowed by Albert Pujols' big night, Adrian Beltre enjoyed quite a showing, going 4 for 5 with a double while scoring twice and driving in a run.

UNLEASHED

"HOPEFULLY AT THE END OF MY CAREER I CAN LOOK BACK AND SAY, 'WOW, WHAT A GAME IT WAS.'"
—Cardinals first baseman Albert Pujols

"IT WAS JUST a great team win. Everybody contributed. We had good quality at-bats. We just took our game plan out there, and we executed pretty much."

Oh, Albert.

Game 3 was a team effort in the same way that the Model T was. People talk about Henry Ford, not Jimmy from the assembly line. So will it be with No. 5.

Pujols did what only Babe Ruth and Reggie Jackson had before — Ruth did it twice — homering three times and with such might that he ensured his name will long resonate in the same vein as the Bambino's and Mr. October's. Combined, Pujols' blasts traveled 1,226 feet, and it doesn't matter a lick that the last two came after the game was well out of hand. During a time of year when superlatives get thrown around more than they should, it's fair to argue that on Oct. 22, 2011, Albert Pujols enjoyed the best night of any batter in World Series history. "I mean, with Babe and Reggie, that's good company right there," said Cardinals Manager Tony La Russa. "It's the latest example of how great he is. You saw it tonight."

The Cardinals are a stoic team, a trait that seems to trickle down directly from their manager. While skipper Ron Washington jumps up and down at even the slightest provocation in the Rangers' dugout, La Russa has been known to crack a smile every couple of seasons. So to see the way the bench reacted after Pujols' third blast, hugging and screaming and generally acting like children on a sugar rush, it was easy to tell that something special was happening.

"I've seen a lot of great things out of him, but that's got to be at the top of the list," said teammate Matt Holliday. "Three home runs, five hits. He's the best I've ever seen. When he gets three hits, he ends up getting four. When he has four, he gets five. He's really good."

Pujols had already won a ring in 2006 and he seems certain to go down in history as one of the greatest offensive forces that the game has ever seen. None of that changed during Game 3, and none of it was necessary. And while it might be easy to say that his three-homer night cemented the first sentence of his obituary, do you really want to bet against his someday hitting four before all is said and done?

"It's pretty special," Pujols eventually conceded. Ruth and Jackson "were great players, and to do it at this level and on this stage is amazing."

GAME 4
RANGERS 4, CARDINALS 0

THE RANGERS HAD not lost two consecutive games since Aug. 27, and that streak remained solid through Game 4. After his team dropped Game 3 at home, 25-year-old left-hander Derek Holland led the charge to even the Series at two games apiece. Holland, who kept the Cardinals' hitters off-balance all game long, threw a masterpiece. He fell two outs short of a complete-game shutout, but had plenty of reasons to be in good spirits after he did not allow a run on just two hits while striking out seven in 8.1 innings. "When [Manager Ron Washington] came out to get me in the ninth, I said 'Come on, Wash, just let me try to get this double play.' He just laughed and said (imitating the animated Washington), 'Nope, nope, you just look at this crowd reaction you get on the way off the field.'"

To bounce back from the crushing loss in Game 3, the Rangers struck first in Game 4 when Josh Hamilton ripped an RBI double down the right-field line for a 1-0 Rangers lead in the first inning. "Any time you can score first, it's big in this kind of game," Ian Kinsler said.

Mike Napoli iced the game with a three-run homer off reliever Mitchell Boggs, putting the Rangers ahead, 4-0, and largely atoning for the tough night he had in Game 3, when he was thrown out at the plate. "We won 96 games during the regular season because we're balanced," said C.J. Wilson when asked how the team remains so resilient. "We have pitching. We have power. We have speed."

The Rangers also had Derek Holland. And although he took the hill with loads of pressure — a loss meant the Cardinals would take a commanding 3-games-to-1 Series lead — the youngster was more than up to the task, unleashing one of the cleanest pitching performances in World Series history. "I knew I had to be really prepared, especially since things hadn't gone so well in a couple other starts," Holland said. "I feel like I did a good job of that. And Napoli did a great job behind the plate. Tonight was huge. I knew I had to step up."

	1	2	3	4	5	6	7	8	9	R	H	E
ST. LOUIS	0	0	0	0	0	0	0	0	0	0	2	0
TEXAS	1	0	0	0	0	3	0	0	x	4	6	0

WP: Holland LP: Jackson
HR: TEX: Napoli

Lance Berkman (left) and Josh Hamilton, representing the St. Louis Rams and Dallas Cowboys, respectively, took part in the coin toss before the Oct. 23 game.

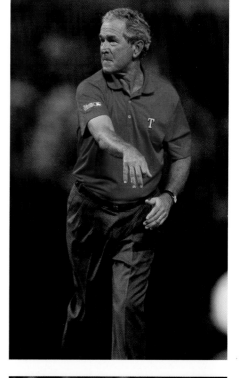

Clockwise from above: Starting in the World Series for the first time, Derek Holland remained in control for 8.1 innings, keeping the Cardinals scoreless; President George W. Bush threw out the ceremonial first pitch; and actress/musician Zooey Deschanel sang the national anthem.

"'HOGGY' [CLUBHOUSE MANAGER RICHARD PRICE] GAVE ME THIS LETTER OPENER THAT LOOKS LIKE A SMALL SWORD BEFORE THE GAME AND SAID, 'HERE, YOU'RE GOING TO WAR.' I WAS LIKE, 'WOW, A LETTER OPENER. THAT'S GOING TO MOTIVATE ME BIG-TIME.'"

—Rangers pitcher Derek Holland

GAME 4
RANGERS 4, CARDINALS 0

"YOU HAVE TO EXPECT THE GUY'S BEST SHOT. YOU CAN'T COME IN THINKING ABOUT HIS LAST COUPLE OF OUTINGS BEING SHAKY. YOU HAVE TO TRY TO PREPARE FOR THE BEST DEREK HOLLAND YOU CAN GET, AND UNFORTUNATELY WE GOT HIM." —Cardinals outfielder Matt Holliday

ANYONE'S GAME

"THAT'S WHY THEY say momentum's only as good as the next day's starting pitcher," Lance Berkman said after the Rangers tied up the World Series, winning Game 4 by a score of 4-0. A night after they hit what seemed like 47 balls into the Rangers Ballpark stands, the Cardinals weren't able to get the win that would have put them on the brink of another title. With the Series split at two games apiece, the Texas win guaranteed a return trip to St. Louis for at least a Game 6, despite the fact that the Rangers, entering the fourth tilt, had held the lead for just one inning during the first three games.

Amazingly, baseball hadn't seen a World Series tied after Game 4 since 2003, when the Yankees and Marlins split the first four. That year, Florida won Game 5 at home, then went on the road to secure the Commissioner's Trophy in Game 6.

So while Rangers fans were thrilled by Mike Napoli's home run, and Cardinals fans were fretting about all of the walks allowed in Game 4 — eight to be precise, including the two that immediately preceded Napoli's sixth-inning at-bat — neutral observers likely had something else on their minds: This was shaping up to be one heck of a compelling finish.

"Now we know it's a great Series," Kinsler said after Game 4. "It's tiring. Every day, you get home and you're just ready for the pillow. Then you wake up ready to come do it again."

Entering 2011, the most recent World Series Game 7 was all the way back in 2002, when the Angels knocked off the Giants for the title (the previous year's Fall Classic also went seven, ending in dramatic fashion when Arizona's Luis Gonzalez blooped the Series-winning hit off the Yankees' Mariano Rivera). But after Game 4 in Texas, there were plenty of people wondering if this Series might go the distance. "I don't know what a seven-game series feels like," Matt Holliday said. "But this feels like a good series."

Clockwise from above: Lance Berkman notched the Cardinals' only two hits of the night; Edwin Jackson held the Rangers to just one run through five innings; Mike Napoli got an ovation after his three-run homer; and fans rose from their seats to show support for the Stand Up to Cancer program.

GAME 5
RANGERS 4, CARDINALS 2

THROUGHOUT THE 2011 postseason, the fans at Rangers Ballpark had been making quite a name for themselves. The stadium was constantly loud, resonating with everything from standard cheers to blaring music to sing-alongs of Texas anthems. So when Mike Napoli stepped into the batter's box with the bases loaded and the score tied in the eighth inning of Game 5, the stadium's decibel level was predictably off the charts.

After the backstop roped a double to the wall in right-center, plating the eventual winning runs, that volume reached rocket-launch heights — a sonic boom

	1	2	3	4	5	6	7	8	9	R	H	E
ST. LOUIS	0	2	0	0	0	0	0	0	0	2	7	1
TEXAS	0	0	1	0	0	1	0	2	x	4	9	2

WP: Oliver **LP:** Dotel **SV:** Feliz
HR: TEX: Moreland, Beltre

Yadier Molina was clearly comfortable at the plate, notching three singles.

that undoubtedly confused people hearing it in Grenada. The two runs upped the score to 4-2, and when Neftali Feliz nailed down a tricky save in the top of the ninth, the Rangers, who had trailed for most of the game, found themselves a win away from the first world title in franchise history as the Series moved back to St. Louis.

"They're really loud. I love our fans," Rangers shortstop Elvis Andrus said of the reaction to Napoli's hit. "They've been like that the whole year, and they always give that extra energy to go out there. It didn't matter if we were down; we believed in ourselves that we could come through."

After the game, much of the talk centered on the two managers and some unusual choices. Rangers skipper Ron Washington won a game despite issuing four intentional walks (three to Albert Pujols), something no manager had ever accomplished in the World Series. But things were even more irregular in the other dugout, where the famous noise created confusion on the bullpen phones, leading to a situation in which the wrong pitchers were warming up and leaving Manager Tony La Russa in a bind. The Cards' skipper had to use a left-hander (Marc Rzepczynski) to face Napoli, despite the fact that right-handers had an OPS more than .270 points higher than lefties against Rzepczynski during the regular season. There was also a miscommunication during a Pujols at-bat in the seventh inning, when Allen Craig was gunned down on a botched hit-and-run (Craig also was caught stealing with Pujols at the plate in the ninth, despite the fact that he represented the non-tying run with a two-run deficit).

It was a bizarre game all around, hardly artistic to say the least. Rangers starter C.J. Wilson had to gut his way through six tough innings with nothing close to his best stuff. Two walks and sloppy play in the second led to two Cardinals runs, and for a while, with Game 1 winner Chris Carpenter dominating on the bump, it seemed like the lead would hold up. But Mitch Moreland homered for Texas in the third and Adrian Beltre added a solo shot in the sixth to tie it. And after Napoli's heroics, the Rangers said goodbye to their home ballpark, forced to leave behind the huge fan support they had so enjoyed while playing in Arlington.

"That's a great way to go," second baseman Ian Kinsler said. "It's the last home game of the season, an unbelievable game in front of this crowd. They got to see the best of us, and it's a great way to end the season at home."

"WINNING TWO STRAIGHT IS GOING TO BE A DIFFICULT TASK, BUT WE'RE NOT GOING TO LAY DOWN. I'LL SAY THIS: IT AIN'T OVER." —Cardinals pitcher Chris Carpenter

Chris Carpenter (top) pitched well, but it wasn't enough. David Murphy's diving catch of a Nick Punto offering with a runner on second base in the top of the second (above) ended the inning, snuffing out a Cardinals rally that had already accounted for two runs in that frame.

GAME 5
RANGERS 4, CARDINALS 2

A PUNCHER'S CHANCE

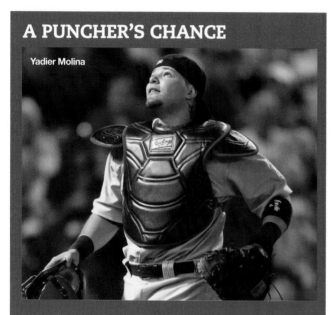

Yadier Molina

DOWN, BUT NOT out. The Cardinals lived by that motto all season long, so naturally a sense of panic was the last thing on players' minds after falling behind in the Series, 3 games to 2. "Nothing changes," said Yadier Molina, who went 3 for 4 with an RBI in Game 5. "We played well, and we played hard so there's nothing to feel sorry about. Now we go back to St. Louis."

Adversity came as no stranger to this club. The Cardinals lost ace starting pitcher Adam Wainwright in Spring Training and went long stretches without both Albert Pujols and Matt Holliday during the season. In September, they set a Major League record — which was trumped just hours later by the Rays — by overcoming an 8.5-game deficit to earn a playoff berth on the season's dramatic final day. "We never make it easy," Jason Motte said. "We haven't made it easy this whole season. We've had our backs against the wall."

After St. Louis hitters collected just one hit in 12 at-bats with runners in scoring position and left 12 men on base in Game 5, their backs were pressed up against that proverbial wall one more time. The fact that the Rangers hadn't lost two consecutive games since late August made the road ahead look even tougher, but try convincing anyone in a Cardinals uniform that it mattered. "We are confident," said Octavio Dotel, who took the loss in relief in Game 5. "We believe in ourselves. We are looking forward to this challenge. We've been in tougher situations than this. We're going to do it. We just need to win two games, and I believe we'll be celebrating at home."

> "I THINK WE ALL KNOW THAT MIKE NAPOLI HAS BEEN ONE OF THE BEST PLAYERS IN BASEBALL SINCE THE ALL-STAR GAME. HE'S BEEN HOT WITH THE BAT, HE'S BEEN AMAZING THROWING BEHIND THE PLATE. HE'S BEEN GREAT CALLING GAMES, TOO. I DON'T KNOW IF HE'S RUNNING FOR PRESIDENT IN 2012, BUT I'LL VOTE FOR HIM."
> —Rangers pitcher C.J. Wilson

Counter-clockwise from above: Adrian Beltre swung so hard on his sixth-inning home run that it brought him to his knee; Skip Schumaker, the Cards' starting center fielder for Game 5, drove in a run in the second and singled later in the game; and Octavio Dotel faced three batters, striking out one.

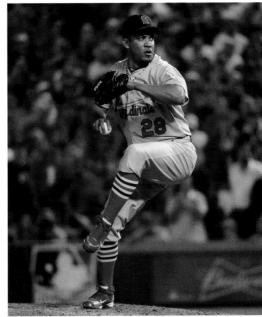

GAME 6
CARDINALS 10, RANGERS 9

"THERE WAS NO tomorrow, and now there is a tomorrow." That's how Albert Pujols summed up one of the greatest, most back-and-forth, exhilarating nights in World Series history. Sure, it had its mishaps. In fact, for the first seven innings, there were five errors, nine walks and two wild pitches. But luckily for fans of America's pastime, Game 6 saved its best for last.

The Rangers started the see-saw affair when Josh Hamilton ripped an RBI single in the first inning, but it

	1	2	3	4	5	6	7	8	9	10	11		R	H	E
TEX	1	1	0	1	1	0	3	0	0	2	0		9	15	2
STL	2	0	0	1	0	1	0	1	2	2	1		10	13	3

WP: Westbrook LP: Lowe
HR: TEX: Beltre, Cruz, Hamilton;
STL: Berkman, Craig, Freese

Lance Berkman had a 3-for-5 night, including a game-tying single in the 10th.

didn't take long for the Cardinals to answer back with a two-run homer from Lance Berkman in the bottom half of the opening frame.

From there, the lead changed hands a remarkable seven times and was tied on five occasions. "I don't know if there is a baseball game better than this one," said Cardinals right-hander Jake Westbrook, who earned the victory after throwing a scoreless 11th inning. "It was great to be a part of."

Although the miscues had piled up by the end of this amazing contest, the lasting image will be of David Freese circling the bases after launching an 11th-inning Mark Lowe change-up over the center-field fence for a walk-off, 10-9 victory. Heroes were in full supply on this night. Hamilton crushed a go-ahead two-run homer in the 10th. Berkman went 3 for 5, reaching base five times, scoring four runs and driving in another three. Adrian Beltre and Nelson Cruz launched back-to-back longballs in the seventh. "It's unbelievable," said hurler Derek Holland, who worked two innings in relief for the Rangers. "I could have had, like, 20 heart attacks. It was like a tennis match."

And Freese was set-point-match. It can't be forgotten that he had already tied the game with a down-to-the-last-strike two-run triple in the ninth inning. Who would have thought that he could top himself just two innings later? "My text inbox is lighting up pretty good," a wide-eyed Freese said after saving his team's season twice in a span of less than 30 minutes. "Going around the bases, I could barely hear anything. I've never hit a walk-off home run in my life. Never. I've never had my teammates waiting for me at home plate."

The best part about the game — one that will go down among the most remarkable ever — wasn't the number 10 or the number 9 that were recorded on the scoreboard, but instead the number 7. Thanks to this remarkable contest, a World Series that already had been one of the most compelling in years would automatically establish itself as a true Fall Classic by reaching the winner-take-all Game 7. How fitting that Game 6 was the 13th one-run game of the 2011 postseason, a new record for close calls. And there's no better way to reach the season's climax than with a seventh game of the World Series. "To go to a Game 7 is unbelievable," Pujols said. "Especially the way we did it tonight. No matter where baseball fans were, they're going to remember this game."

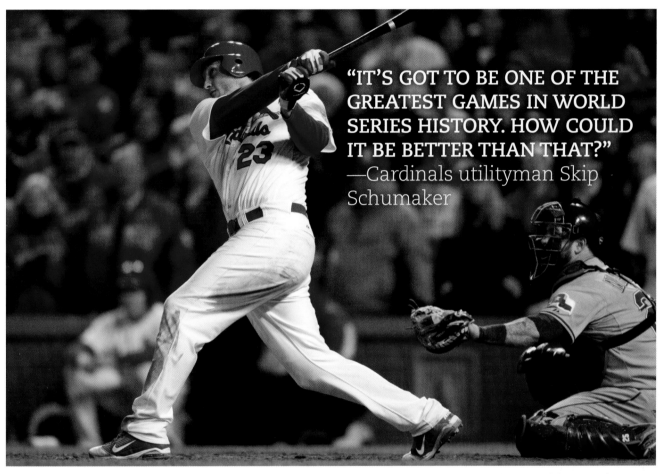

"IT'S GOT TO BE ONE OF THE GREATEST GAMES IN WORLD SERIES HISTORY. HOW COULD IT BE BETTER THAN THAT?"
—Cardinals utilityman Skip Schumaker

The hero of the night, David Freese (above), made his two hits count, with a game-tying triple in the bottom of the ninth to send the contest into extra innings and later the walk-off homer. His Cardinals teammates bounded out of the dugout to greet him at the plate in the bottom of the 11th.

GAME 6
CARDINALS 10, RANGERS 9

"WE FELT LIKE WE HAD THE GAME WON. BUT WE KNOW HOW THINGS WORK. YOU'VE GOT TO GET THAT FINAL OUT."

—Rangers first baseman Michael Young

BEAUTY IS PAIN

WHAT NEEDS TO be remembered is that the end of Game 6 of the 2011 World Series was baseball at its absolute best. What maybe ought to be forgotten is everything that happened in the first seven frames.

And yet, in a way, it really was the whole package — the errors and the dazzling plays, the strikeouts and the home runs, the highs and the lows — that should forever define what was one of the greatest, most exhilarating World Series games of all time. Twice, St. Louis found itself down to its last strike, and, respectfully, there wasn't a red-clad fan in the stands who didn't realize that the team had brought that upon itself. Three errors in the first five innings, enough walks to get across the Mississippi and back, and pitchers who kept giving back whatever momentum the offense had created. In truth, when the Rangers' Elvis Andrus popped out to end the fourth, stranding two more runners on base, it was pretty remarkable that the Cardinals still managed to be within one run — in a just world, the Rangers would have been leading by a margin of about 12 by then. "You know, it's not that easy to win a world championship, as we found out tonight," Rangers Manager Ron Washington said.

But over on the Cardinals' side of the field, no matter how bleak things looked and no matter how many balls were being kicked around, the fact remained that, as long as it stayed tight and they had outs left, there was no time for panic.

"It wasn't a perfect game defensively for both of us," Cardinals Manager Tony La Russa said afterward, "and sure, we botched a couple of fly balls that led to runs, but as long as the score is [close] ... As soon as the guys came off the field, I heard it 10 times — 'nine outs.' So I mean, the guys were into it. That's what happens when you give yourself a shot. Hard way to go. I would prefer not to do it this way."

There are going to be a lot of people calling Game 6 one of the greatest in baseball history, and since declarations like that are fun, there's no reason to remind them of the miscues and slip-ups that preceded the perfection. The penultimate game of the 2011 Fall Classic wasn't always a knockout. It wasn't even always average. Okay, fine, it was downright unsightly at times. But the end was so, so, so good. And you'll never forget it. "Really, truly, this was an ugly game for about six or seven innings," Lance Berkman, one of about a dozen Cardinals heroes, said after the game. "But then it got really pretty."

Clockwise from above left: Josh Hamilton's 10th-inning homer put Texas on top again, while Nelson Cruz's bomb added an insurance run in the seventh; Lance Berkman's first-inning blast reached the seats; and Yadier Molina drew a bases-loaded walk in the sixth to plate a run.

GAME 7
CARDINALS 6, RANGERS 2

GOING INTO THE Series' final night, one team hadn't lost two straight games since August, but suffered a crushing loss in Game 6. The other had fought back and overcome adversity all season, but was throwing its ace pitcher on short rest. The Rangers and Cardinals each looked like unstoppable teams of destiny. Something had to give.

Game 7 picked up right where the historic Game 6 had left off. Ian Kinsler — who has reached base in 31 of his first 33 career playoff games — started off with a single,

	1	2	3	4	5	6	7	8	9	R	H	E
TEXAS	2	0	0	0	0	0	0	0	0	2	6	0
ST. LOUIS	2	0	1	0	2	0	1	0	x	6	7	1

WP: Carpenter LP: Harrison
HR: STL: Craig

David Freese took home the Fall Classic MVP Award after going 8 for 23 with seven RBI and four runs scored during the Series.

as he often does, and was doubled in by Josh Hamilton. Michael Young added an RBI double of his own, and Texas had a quick 2-0 lead. So much for feeling devastated from the night before. "The Rangers were tough every step of the way," said Allen Craig. "They didn't quit at any point."

But the Cardinals, too, refused to fold. After Rangers starter Matt Harrison walked two batters in the bottom of the first, Game 6 hero David Freese did it again — lacing a two-run double into the left-field gap to tie the score, 2-2.

Craig, who came off the bench to belt an eighth-inning homer in Game 6, got the Game 7 start in left field because of Matt Holliday's hand injury and put St. Louis ahead with a solo home run in the bottom of the third. From there, the Cardinals took control of the game, starting with the settling down of their ace, Chris Carpenter. "After the first inning, I was able to get ahead, control the count and I was able to get my breaking ball over," Carpenter said.

Once Carpenter settled down, the Cards tacked on runs when the Rangers' bullpen failed to find the strike zone. Scott Feldman walked Yadier Molina to force home a run in the fifth, then C.J. Wilson entered and beaned Rafael Furcal to push across another. Four St. Louis relievers combined to throw three scoreless frames, as the Texas bats were held virtually silent after the first inning. Molina added an RBI single in the seventh, and St. Louis was on its way to its 11th world title — the second in the past six seasons.

Although the final game of 2011 ultimately fell short of the theatrics in Game 6 — and how could it not? — this Series as a whole will forever be among the most compelling. Just reaching Game 7 guaranteed this Fall Classic some historical value, and the tightly contested, up-and-down affairs made it even more unforgettable. "I'm really proud to be the commissioner of a sport that can produce what just happened," Commissioner Bud Selig said following Game 6. "Just to get up this morning and hear people say, 'It's Game 7 of the World Series' is a thrill."

The 2011 regular season ended with one of the wildest nights in history, then the dramatics continued. Just three games under the maximum were played in the three postseason rounds combined — 38 out of a possible 41, tied with 2003 for the most ever. So, of course, this Fall Classic had to go seven games, and the most resilient team remained standing at the end. "I think the last month of the season, that's what started everything," said Albert Pujols. "Different guys were coming up huge. It was an amazing season, and here we are — we're world champions."

> "OUR BALLCLUB HERE IS UNBELIEVABLE. YOU DO NOT EVEN KNOW THE KIND OF QUALITY PEOPLE WE HAVE."
> —Cardinals pitcher Chris Carpenter

Clockwise from above: After giving up two runs in the first to get the win, Chris Carpenter threw five shutout innings; left fielder Allen Craig robbed Nelson Cruz of a home run with an over-the-wall catch in the sixth inning; and starter Matt Harrison couldn't get it done for Texas, giving up three runs.

GAME 7
CARDINALS 6, RANGERS 2

"THAT'S PROBABLY THE WAY TO EXPLAIN THIS: UNBELIEVABLE, AMAZING, INCREDIBLE."
—Cardinals Manager Tony La Russa

DEEP FREESE

DAVID FREESE REVEALED his aspirations early in the World Series. After Game 1, he told a story about watching Cardinals playoff games as a kid while growing up in nearby Wildwood, Mo. He discussed with teammates the fact that he'd like to see photos of the 2011 Cardinals on the wall next to those of past championship squads. David Freese has officially earned his way onto the wall.

"This means everything," Freese said of the World Series victory. "This team deserves this. This organization is top-notch and these fans are unbelievable — definitely the best fans in baseball."

Freese batted .348 (8 for 23) in the World Series on his way to MVP honors. His production included three doubles, a triple, a home run and seven RBI. He finished October with 21 RBI, which set a new record for a single postseason.

"Nobody deserves this success more than David," said Albert Pujols. "He's one of the nicest guys in the league."

The Cardinals' third baseman collected at least one base hit in all but one of the first five games. Then came his signature moment — actually, two signature moments in the late innings of Game 6. With the Cardinals down by two runs, two men on base and Freese down to his last strike, he lofted a two-run triple

off the right-field wall. As he dove into third base and saved the Cardinals' season, he gave club executives one option for the photo that will go up on that wall to depict the 2011 postseason. Two innings later, he created an even better photo opp. With the score tied, 9-9, in the bottom of the 11th, Freese drove a ball far over the center-field fence to end one of the most topsy-turvy Fall Classic games ever played.

"When it left, I started thinking about Jim Edmonds/Game 6 a little bit, I have to admit," Freese said. In 2004, the then-Cardinals slugger launched a walk-off, 12th-inning home run to end Game 6 of that year's NLCS against Houston. Ironically, Freese was traded to the Cardinals from the Padres for Jim Edmonds — one of his childhood heroes — in 2007.

After a two-run, game-tying double in the first inning of Game 7, Freese had already locked up the fact that he would become the sixth player ever to win an LCS and World Series MVP award in the same season. "I'm trying to soak this all in," he said. "You never know if it's your last attempt at a title. If we had lost tonight, we were still NL champs and did a ton that nobody thought we could accomplish. And then to win it is an incredible feeling."

Clockwise from above left: Fans in St. Louis celebrated their club's Fall Classic triumph over the Rangers; Jason Motte recorded a 1-2-3 ninth inning to shut down Texas for the win; and the 2011 world champion Cardinals received the franchise's 11th World Series trophy.

NO.	PLAYER	B/T	G	W	L	IP	ERA	SO	BB	WHIP	SV
PITCHERS											
41	Mitchell Boggs	R/R	7	0	0	7.2	5.87	5	2	1.57	0
29	Chris Carpenter	R/R	6	4	0	36.0	3.25	21	11	1.17	0
28	Octavio Dotel	R/R	12	2	1	10.1	2.61	14	2	0.68	0
54	Jaime Garcia	L/L	5	0	2	25.2	4.21	21	8	1.36	0
22	Edwin Jackson	R/R	4	1	1	17.2	5.60	12	9	1.58	0
26	Kyle Lohse	R/R	3	0	2	12.2	7.82	10	3	1.66	0
62	Lance Lynn	R/R	10	2	0	11.0	3.27	5	5	1.36	0
46	Kyle McClellan	R/R	1	0	0	0.1	27.00	0	0	6.00	0
30	Jason Motte	R/R	12	0	1	12.1	2.19	8	1	0.49	5
53	Arthur Rhodes	L/L	8	0	0	2.2	0.00	3	1	0.37	0
34	Marc Rzepczynski	L/L	12	1	0	8.1	4.32	9	1	0.96	0
59	Fernando Salas	R/R	11	0	0	13.1	3.38	12	4	1.20	0
35	Jake Westbrook	R/R	2	1	0	2.0	0.00	0	1	1.50	0

NO.	PLAYER	B/T	G	AB	H	AVG	HR	RBI	OBP	SLG	SB
CATCHERS											
13	Gerald Laird	R/R	4	1	0	.000	0	0	.000	.000	0
4	Yadier Molina	R/R	18	67	20	.299	0	12	.360	.373	1
INFIELDERS											
33	Daniel Descalso	L/R	13	9	3	.333	0	0	.333	.333	0
23	David Freese	R/R	18	63	25	.397	5	21	.465	.794	0
15	Rafael Furcal	S/R	18	77	15	.195	1	3	.244	.325	1
5	Albert Pujols	R/R	18	68	24	.353	5	16	.463	.691	1
8	Nick Punto	S/R	15	35	6	.171	0	3	.302	.171	0
55	Skip Schumaker	L/R	11	21	8	.381	0	4	.381	.476	0
3	Ryan Theriot	R/R	12	33	8	.242	0	3	.265	.303	1
OUTFIELDERS											
12	Lance Berkman	S/L	18	64	20	.313	2	11	.413	.438	2
56	Adron Chambers	L/L	10	5	1	.200	0	2	.167	.200	0
21	Allen Craig	R/R	15	37	9	.243	4	8	.391	.622	0
7	Matt Holliday	R/R	16	51	15	.294	1	5	.419	.412	0
19	Jon Jay	L/L	18	55	10	.182	0	3	.262	.218	1

POSTSEASON HISTORY

The 1934 Cardinals, also known as the Gashouse Gang, were pushed to the brink in the World Series, but crushed Detroit in Game 7 for the world title.

1926*
WORLD SERIES

IN THE 1880s, the Cardinals — then known as the Brown Stockings — were immensely successful as members of the American Association, winning four pennants in 10 years before entering the National League. For a period after joining the NL, though, they could not match their previous success and struggled to contend.

In 1919, the team hired Branch Rickey, who established baseball's first farm system while in St. Louis. That paid dividends quickly, and the Cardinals became one of the National League's most successful teams. This run started in 1926, when the Redbirds — led by Les Bell and future Hall of Famer Rogers Hornsby — defeated Babe Ruth and Lou Gehrig's Yankees in seven games to capture their first of many World Series crowns.

CARDINALS 4, NEW YORK YANKEES 3
Oct. 2 Cardinals 1 at Yankees 2
Oct. 3 Cardinals 6 at Yankees 2
Oct. 5 Yankees 0 at Cardinals 4
Oct. 6 Yankees 10 at Cardinals 5
Oct. 7 Yankees 3 at Cardinals 2
Oct. 9 Cardinals 10 at Yankees 2
Oct. 10 Cardinals 3 at Yankees 2

1928
WORLD SERIES
NEW YORK YANKEES 4, CARDINALS 0
Oct. 4 Cardinals 1 at Yankees 4
Oct. 5 Cardinals 3 at Yankees 9
Oct. 7 Yankees 7 at Cardinals 3
Oct. 9 Yankees 7 at Cardinals 3

1930
WORLD SERIES
PHILADELPHIA ATHLETICS 4, CARDINALS 2
Oct. 1 Cardinals 2 at Athletics 5
Oct. 2 Cardinals 1 at Athletics 6
Oct. 4 Athletics 0 at Cardinals 5
Oct. 5 Athletics 1 at Cardinals 3
Oct. 6 Athletics 2 at Cardinals 0
Oct. 8 Cardinals 1 at Athletics 7

1931*
WORLD SERIES
THE PHILADELPHIA ATHLETICS were something of a juggernaut in 1931. With Jimmie Foxx on the verge of becoming one of baseball's elite hitters and Lefty Grove in

*Denotes Championship Season

the midst of a Hall-of-Fame career, the two-time-defending-world-champion A's won 107 games and cruised to the World Series, winning the American League pennant by a staggering 13.5 games.

The Cards, though, were ready to make history of their own and avenge their loss in the previous season's Series.

After the A's forced a Game 7 in St. Louis, the Redbirds came out hot, scoring two in the first and two in the third and giving Burleigh Grimes more than enough support, as he kept Philadelphia off the board until the ninth and held on for the 4-2 win.

CARDINALS 4, PHILADELPHIA ATHLETICS 3
Oct. 1 Athletics 6 at Cardinals 2
Oct. 2 Athletics 0 at Cardinals 2
Oct. 5 Cardinals 5 at Athletics 2
Oct. 6 Cardinals 0 at Athletics 3
Oct. 7 Cardinals 5 at Athletics 1
Oct. 9 Athletics 8 at Cardinals 1
Oct. 10 Athletics 2 at Cardinals 4

1934*
WORLD SERIES

AFTER WINNING THE 1931 World Series, the Cardinals fell off the map for a bit. The team failed to finish in the top half of the league in each of the next two seasons and did not appear poised for any kind of title run. But with great campaigns from future Hall of Famers Dizzy Dean and Joe Medwick, St. Louis was back in the Fall Classic in 1934.

The Hank Greenberg–led Tigers secured a 3-games-to-2 Series advantage over St. Louis before coming home for Games 6 and 7. Home field didn't prove much of an advantage, though, as pitcher Paul Dean delivered a game-winning single in Game 6. His brother Dizzy then took the mound in Game 7 and finished off the Series with a shutout, giving the Cardinals their third championship.

CARDINALS 4, DETROIT TIGERS 3
Oct. 3 Cardinals 8 at Tigers 3
Oct. 4 Cardinals 2 at Tigers 3 (12 innings)
Oct. 5 Tigers 1 at Cardinals 4
Oct. 6 Tigers 10 at Cardinals 4
Oct. 7 Tigers 3 at Cardinals 1
Oct. 8 Cardinals 4 at Tigers 3
Oct. 9 Cardinals 11 at Tigers 0

1942*
WORLD SERIES

THE CARDINALS BEGAN an incredible string of success in the 1940s by beating the Joe DiMaggio–led Yankees in just five games, including the final four in a row, to earn their fourth World Series title.

The club won 106 regular-season games and featured future Hall of Famers Stan Musial and Enos Slaughter, who helped supply enough hitting to beat the 103-win Yankees.

Lights-out pitching helped the Cardinals control the Series, as the staff allowed just 13 earned runs in the five games. After the Game 1 loss, the vaunted Yankees offense scored more than three runs just once and was shut out by Ernie White in Game 3.

The dominant Series win proved to be a sign of things to come for a team on the rise.

CARDINALS 4, NEW YORK YANKEES 1
Sept. 30 Yankees 7 at Cardinals 4
Oct. 1 Yankees 3 at Cardinals 4
Oct. 3 Cardinals 2 at Yankees 0
Oct. 4 Cardinals 9 at Yankees 6
Oct. 5 Cardinals 4 at Yankees 2

1943
WORLD SERIES
NEW YORK YANKEES 4, CARDINALS 1
Oct. 5 Cardinals 2 at Yankees 4
Oct. 6 Cardinals 4 at Yankees 3
Oct. 7 Cardinals 2 at Yankees 6
Oct. 10 Yankees 2 at Cardinals 1
Oct. 11 Yankees 2 at Cardinals 0

1944*
WORLD SERIES

AFTER MAKING TWO consecutive World Series trips, the Cardinals were prepared for another extended season in 1944. Fortunately, they didn't have to travel at all, as they matched up against their intra-city rivals, the Browns, in the Fall Classic. Each game was played at Sportsman's Park.

The light-hitting Browns, who came out of nowhere to win the American League, took two of the first three games in the Series. But the Cardinals rebounded to win the final three contests, riding Stan Musial's hot bat to their second championship in three years. They remain the last National League team to win the pennant in three consecutive years.

CARDINALS 4, ST. LOUIS BROWNS 2
Oct. 4 Browns 2 at Cardinals 1
Oct. 5 Browns 2 at Cardinals 3 (11 innings)
Oct. 6 Cardinals 2 at Browns 6
Oct. 7 Cardinals 5 at Browns 1
Oct. 8 Cardinals 2 at Browns 0
Oct. 9 Browns 1 at Cardinals 3

1946*
WORLD SERIES

THE 1946 FALL Classic featured a showdown between two of baseball's best bats in Boston's Ted Williams and St. Louis's Stan Musial. But even though the two sluggers did not end up producing quite as expected, the Series didn't disappoint, going the full slate. Facing a 3-games-to-2 deficit after losing Game 5, the Cards came home to win the next one and set up a dramatic Game 7 in St. Louis.

In Game 7, the Red Sox made a late charge to tie the contest, 3-3, in the eighth inning, but the Cards quickly responded when Harry Walker doubled to score Enos Slaughter, whose "mad dash" from first base proved to be the difference in the World Series.

CARDINALS 4, BOSTON RED SOX 3
Oct. 6 Red Sox 3 at Cardinals 2 (10 innings)
Oct. 7 Red Sox 0 at Cardinals 3
Oct. 9 Cardinals 0 at Red Sox 4
Oct. 10 Cardinals 12 at Red Sox 3
Oct. 11 Cardinals 3 at Red Sox 6
Oct. 13 Red Sox 1 at Cardinals 4
Oct. 15 Red Sox 3 at Cardinals 4

1964*
WORLD SERIES

DESPITE FACING THE powerful Yankees, who featured Mickey Mantle, Roger Maris, Elston Howard and Whitey Ford, the Cardinals were up to the challenge, especially after overcoming a 6.5-game deficit with 13 games to play just to make the Fall Classic.

In a back-and-forth Series, the Cardinals relied on that resiliency to bounce back from a Game 6 loss and beat the Yankees in Game 7 behind Bob Gibson and an offensive explosion that included home runs from Lou Brock

and Ken Boyer, as well as Tim McCarver stealing home on a double steal. This offense proved to be more than enough, as Gibson, despite facing pressure in the ninth, held on for the 7-5 win and earned the Series MVP Award.

CARDINALS 4, NEW YORK YANKEES 3
Oct. 7 Yankees 5 at Cardinals 9
Oct. 8 Yankees 8 at Cardinals 3
Oct. 10 Cardinals 1 at Yankees 2
Oct. 11 Cardinals 4 at Yankees 3
Oct. 12 Cardinals 5 at Yankees 2 (10 innings)
Oct. 14 Yankees 8 at Cardinals 3
Oct. 15 Yankees 5 at Cardinals 7

1967*
WORLD SERIES

TO WIN A World Series, it usually takes a team effort. Bob Gibson is a special case, though; he might have been able to do it all by himself in 1967.

After winning 101 games in the regular season, the Cardinals looked poised to take it all, but the Red Sox, led by Triple Crown winner Carl Yastrzemski, triumphed in Games 5 and 6 to force a decisive Game 7.

Luckily for St. Louis, Gibson took the hill. After dominating in Games 1 and 4, giving up one run in 18 innings, Gibson did come through once more. He would go the distance and shut down the Sox offense, throwing his third complete game of the Series and allowing just two runs in the Fall Classic–clinching win.

CARDINALS 4, BOSTON RED SOX 3
Oct. 4 Cardinals 2 at Red Sox 1
Oct. 5 Cardinals 0 at Red Sox 5
Oct. 7 Red Sox 2 at Cardinals 5
Oct. 8 Red Sox 0 at Cardinals 6
Oct. 9 Red Sox 3 at Cardinals 1
Oct. 11 Cardinals 4 at Red Sox 8
Oct. 12 Cardinals 7 at Red Sox 2

1968
WORLD SERIES
DETROIT TIGERS 4, CARDINALS 3
Oct. 2 Tigers 0 at Cardinals 4
Oct. 3 Tigers 8 at Cardinals 1
Oct. 5 Cardinals 7 at Tigers 3
Oct. 6 Cardinals 10 at Tigers 1

*Denotes Championship Season

Oct. 7 Cardinals 3 at Tigers 5
Oct. 9 Tigers 13 at Cardinals 1
Oct. 10 Tigers 4 at Cardinals 1

1982*
NLCS
CARDINALS 3, ATLANTA BRAVES 0
Oct. 7 Braves 0 at Cardinals 7
Oct. 9 Braves 3 at Cardinals 4
Oct. 10 Cardinals 6 at Braves 2

WORLD SERIES

The Cardinals squashed the Brewers' title hopes in the 1982 Fall Classic.

GOING INTO THE 1982 season, the Cardinals had long ago established themselves as one of baseball's most successful franchises, but even the best clubs experience droughts, and theirs had reached 14 seasons. Since their loss in the 1968 World Series, they had struggled to even contend. The tides turned in the 1982 season, though, when the Cardinals did more than compete, as they took down Harvey's Wallbangers in seven games in the World Series. The Cardinals faced elimination after the Brewers won Game 5 to take the Series lead, but they had the good fortune of returning to their home ballpark for the final two contests.

The Cards took Game 6, 13-1, and then, behind ace Joaquin Andujar, rallied for three runs in the sixth inning on singles from Keith Hernandez and George Hendrick to take a 4-3 lead, which would prove to be enough as the Redbirds eventually won, 6-3.

CARDINALS 4, MILWAUKEE BREWERS 3
Oct. 12 Brewers 10 at Cardinals 0
Oct. 13 Brewers 4 at Cardinals 5

Oct. 15 Cardinals 6 at Brewers 2
Oct. 16 Cardinals 5 at Brewers 7
Oct. 17 Cardinals 4 at Brewers 6
Oct. 19 Brewers 1 at Cardinals 13
Oct. 20 Brewers 3 at Cardinals 6

1985
NLCS
CARDINALS 4, LOS ANGELES DODGERS 2
Oct. 9 Cardinals 1 at Dodgers 4
Oct. 10 Cardinals 2 at Dodgers 8
Oct. 12 Dodgers 2 at Cardinals 4
Oct. 13 Dodgers 2 at Cardinals 12
Oct. 14 Dodgers 2 at Cardinals 3
Oct. 16 Cardinals 7 at Dodgers 5

WORLD SERIES
KANSAS CITY ROYALS 4, CARDINALS 3
Oct. 19 Cardinals 3 at Royals 1
Oct. 20 Cardinals 4 at Royals 2
Oct. 22 Royals 6 at Cardinals 1
Oct. 23 Royals 0 at Cardinals 3
Oct. 24 Royals 6 at Cardinals 1
Oct. 26 Cardinals 1 at Royals 2
Oct. 27 Cardinals 0 at Royals 11

1987
NLCS
CARDINALS 4, SAN FRANCISCO GIANTS 3
Oct. 6 Giants 3 at Cardinals 5
Oct. 7 Giants 5 at Cardinals 0
Oct. 9 Cardinals 6 at Giants 5
Oct. 10 Cardinals 2 at Giants 4
Oct. 11 Cardinals 3 at Giants 6
Oct. 13 Giants 0 at Cardinals 1
Oct. 14 Giants 0 at Cardinals 6

WORLD SERIES
MINNESOTA TWINS 4, CARDINALS 3
Oct. 17 Cardinals 1 at Twins 10
Oct. 18 Cardinals 4 at Twins 8
Oct. 20 Twins 1 at Cardinals 3
Oct. 21 Twins 2 at Cardinals 7
Oct. 22 Twins 2 at Cardinals 4
Oct. 24 Cardinals 5 at Twins 11
Oct. 25 Cardinals 2 at Twins 4

Albert Pujols and the Cardinals celebrated their 2006 world title.

Scott Rolen and Albert Pujols embraced after the final out of the '06 Series.

1996
NLDS
CARDINALS 3, SAN DIEGO PADRES 0
Oct. 1 Padres 1 at Cardinals 3
Oct. 3 Padres 4 at Cardinals 5
Oct. 5 Cardinals 7 at Padres 5

NLCS
ATLANTA BRAVES 4, CARDINALS 3
Oct. 9 Cardinals 2 at Braves 4
Oct. 10 Cardinals 8 at Braves 3
Oct. 12 Braves 2 at Cardinals 3
Oct. 13 Braves 3 at Cardinals 4
Oct. 14 Braves 14 at Cardinals 0
Oct. 16 Cardinals 1 at Braves 3
Oct. 17 Cardinals 0 at Braves 15

2000
NLDS
CARDINALS 3, ATLANTA BRAVES 0
Oct. 3 Braves 5 at Cardinals 7
Oct. 5 Braves 4 at Cardinals 10
Oct. 7 Cardinals 7 at Braves 1

NLCS
NEW YORK METS 4, CARDINALS 1
Oct. 11 Mets 6 at Cardinals 2
Oct. 12 Mets 6 at Cardinals 5
Oct. 14 Cardinals 8 at Mets 2
Oct. 15 Cardinals 6 at Mets 10
Oct. 16 Cardinals 0 at Mets 7

2001
NLDS
ARIZONA DIAMONDBACKS 3, CARDINALS 2
Oct. 9 Cardinals 0 at Diamondbacks 1
Oct. 10 Cardinals 4 at Diamondbacks 1
Oct. 12 Diamondbacks 5 at Cardinals 3
Oct. 13 Diamondbacks 1 at Cardinals 4
Oct. 14 Cardinals 1 at Diamondbacks 2

2002
NLDS
CARDINALS 3, ARIZONA DIAMONDBACKS 0
Oct. 1 Cardinals 12 at Diamondbacks 2
Oct. 3 Cardinals 2 at Diamondbacks 1
Oct. 5 Diamondbacks 3 at Cardinals 6

NLCS
SAN FRANCISCO GIANTS 4, CARDINALS 1
Oct. 9 Giants 9 at Cardinals 6
Oct. 10 Giants 4 at Cardinals 1
Oct. 12 Cardinals 5 at Giants 4
Oct. 13 Cardinals 3 at Giants 4
Oct. 14 Cardinals 1 at Giants 2

2004
NLDS
CARDINALS 3, LOS ANGELES DODGERS 1
Oct. 5 Dodgers 3 at Cardinals 8
Oct. 7 Dodgers 3 at Cardinals 8
Oct. 9 Cardinals 0 at Dodgers 4
Oct. 10 Cardinals 6 at Dodgers 2

*Denotes Championship Season

NLCS
CARDINALS 4, HOUSTON ASTROS 3
Oct. 13 Astros 7 at Cardinals 10
Oct. 14 Astros 4 at Cardinals 6
Oct. 16 Cardinals 2 at Astros 5
Oct. 17 Cardinals 5 at Astros 6
Oct. 18 Cardinals 0 at Astros 3
Oct. 20 Astros 4 at Cardinals 6 (12 innings)
Oct. 21 Astros 2 at Cardinals 5

WORLD SERIES
BOSTON RED SOX 4, CARDINALS 0
Oct. 23 Cardinals 9 at Red Sox 11
Oct. 24 Cardinals 2 at Red Sox 6
Oct. 26 Red Sox 4 at Cardinals 1
Oct. 27 Red Sox 3 at Cardinals 0

2005
NLDS
CARDINALS 3, SAN DIEGO PADRES 0
Oct. 4 Padres 5 at Cardinals 8
Oct. 6 Padres 2 at Cardinals 6
Oct. 8 Cardinals 7 at Padres 4

NLCS
HOUSTON ASTROS 4, CARDINALS 2
Oct. 12 Astros 3 at Cardinals 5
Oct. 13 Astros 4 at Cardinals 1
Oct. 15 Cardinals 3 at Astros 4
Oct. 16 Cardinals 1 at Astros 2
Oct. 17 Cardinals 5 at Astros 4
Oct. 19 Astros 5 at Cardinals 1

2006*
NLDS
CARDINALS 3, SAN DIEGO PADRES 1
Oct. 3 Cardinals 5 at Padres 1
Oct. 5 Cardinals 2 at Padres 0
Oct. 7 Padres 3 at Cardinals 1
Oct. 8 Padres 2 at Cardinals 6

NLCS
CARDINALS 4, NEW YORK METS 3
Oct. 12 Cardinals 0 at Mets 2
Oct. 13 Cardinals 9 at Mets 6
Oct. 14 Mets 0 at Cardinals 5
Oct. 15 Mets 12 at Cardinals 5
Oct. 17 Mets 2 at Cardinals 4
Oct. 18 Cardinals 2 at Mets 4
Oct. 19 Cardinals 3 at Mets 1

WORLD SERIES
FOLLOWING BACK-TO-BACK 100-WIN seasons that did not result in a World Series championship, the Cardinals were left unfulfilled. Oddly enough, it was a season in which they won just 83 games that would get them back over the hump. Led by the big three of Albert Pujols, Jim Edmonds and Scott Rolen, as well as ace Chris Carpenter and emerging star Adam Wainwright, St. Louis shocked the baseball world and beat the heavily-favored New York Mets in the NLCS to get to the World Series. They then tamed the 95-win Detroit Tigers to win it all. Finally, after years of coming close, Manager Tony La Russa had won a World Series in St. Louis.

CARDINALS 4, DETROIT TIGERS 1
Oct. 21 Cardinals 7 at Tigers 2
Oct. 22 Cardinals 1 at Tigers 3
Oct. 24 Tigers 0 at Cardinals 5
Oct. 26 Tigers 4 at Cardinals 5
Oct. 27 Tigers 2 at Cardinals 4

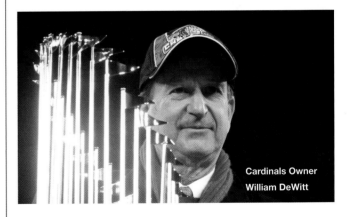

Cardinals Owner
William DeWitt

2009
NLDS
LOS ANGELES DODGERS 3, CARDINALS 0
Oct. 7 Cardinals 3 at Dodgers 5
Oct. 8 Cardinals 2 at Dodgers 3
Oct. 10 Dodgers 5 at Cardinals 1

WORLD SERIES LOGO

THE WORLD SERIES is a brand in itself. Throughout the Fall Classic, the Series logo appears seemingly everywhere: It's sewn onto uniform sleeves, pressed onto hats, stenciled onto playing fields and emblazoned onto countless souvenirs, clothing items and printed materials.

With such a high degree of visibility, MLB puts just as much effort and consideration into the design of each year's World Series logo as it does into any redesign of club-specific logos and uniforms. In both instances, the task falls to Anne Occi, MLB's vice president of design services, and her staff.

The World Series logo must be created about a year in advance and made publicly available by Dec. 1, because much of the World Series–related merchandise is produced ahead of time, and some media outlets like to have the logo to use in season preview magazines and newspaper special sections. Such an advanced schedule can make it difficult to create an icon that will still look timely by the first pitch of the Fall Classic.

That's why Occi subscribes to several trend-forecasting services that have an uncanny ability to predict upcoming design trends, even a year in advance.

"We'll be able to know what colors will be in style and whether the design should be progressive, retro or conservative," Occi said.

By employing trend forecasting, the World Series logo attempts to correspond with the styles of clothing that will be produced for the event. While basic T-shirts vary little, other sportswear evolves, matching better with certain logo styles.

"Certain color waves might be out of style for a particular demographic in menswear or womenswear," Occi said. "With the forecasting, we know we'll be dead-on

with what our licensees will be using and can apply our graphic to."

Even the "World Series" typeset is selected to match the trend forecasting. In 2008, a typeset called ITC Century Handtooled was used, although with some in-house tweaking, it essentially became a hand-drawn font.

The World Series logo was generic until 1978, when a more intricate design was used to celebrate the 75th Fall Classic. The logo stayed the same from 1980 to '86, with just the year updated. The pattern of using a nearly identical logo for several years continued in periods from 1987–91, 1992–97 and 1998–99.

From 2001 through 2007, the World Series logo evolved into a modern, progressive, almost space-age look that focused on the international element of "world," much like the logo for the World Baseball Classic.

For the first time in 2008, the logo included the words "Fall Classic" in smaller print on a red banner below "World Series." Created by MLB designer Erin Sfarra, it also featured a pair of leaves in red and gold, and had a traditional look with a heavy dose of green.

The 2011 logo was the first that did not include blue, and the red used — a brick red similar to that of the Arizona Diamondbacks' and Houston Astros' color palattes — is only a subtle accent color. The MLB logo of a silhouetted batter has only a slight outline in red.

With green and shades of gold, along with larger leaves, the logo looks more festive, almost like a Thanksgiving centerpiece. The "Fall Classic" theme remains.

After sticking with similar World Series logos for the last two decades of the 20th century, MLB's design team now begins each year with a blank slate, building upon design trends to create a logo that's both timely and classic.

THE 2011 LOGO WAS THE FIRST THAT DID NOT INCLUDE BLUE. WITH SHADES OF GOLD, ALONG WITH LARGER LEAVES, THE LOGO LOOKS MORE FESTIVE, ALMOST LIKE A THANKSGIVING CENTERPIECE. THE "FALL CLASSIC" THEME REMAINS.

TICKETING

WORLD SERIES TICKETS are generally very difficult commodites to obtain. The task of regulating who gets them is even more so. But sometimes, more fans than usual get the chance to purchase tickets. That's because season-ticket holders have the right to purchase seats for the Fall Classic. If a team only has a modest base of season-ticket holders, fans are in luck. But in towns like Boston, New York and St. Louis, that base accounts for much of the ballpark.

Another large quantity of tickets, approximately a few thousand for each game, is earmarked for Major League Baseball to allot to sponsors and league officials. Television rights holders — which in the past have included NBC, FOX, ESPN and TBS — also receive an allotment, as do individual teams and the Major League Baseball Players Association.

Players on the two participating teams can purchase up to six tickets each for both home and away games during the Series. All Major League umpires, not just the six working the event, are given the opportunity to buy four per game. But unlike the NFL, in which every player in the league can buy two tickets to the Super Bowl, players on non-participating Major League teams are not given special access to purchase tickets.

Because the task of determining who gets to purchase which tickets can be so complicated and challenging, Rob Capilli, Major League Baseball's senior manager of special events, is assigned full-time to ticketing for baseball's jewel events: the World Series and the rest of the playoffs, the All-Star Game and the World Baseball Classic, not to mention many regular-season games.

Capilli's group contacts all contending teams shortly after the conclusion of the All-Star break to help them formulate their ticketing plans for the World Series. Because of the expanded playoffs that have been in place since 1995, that's usually about 18 teams — a group that gets whittled down to about a dozen with two weeks left in the regular season.

Each contending team must submit a plan to Capilli detailing the allotment of tickets, as well as which seats will be available, since some sections are converted into an auxiliary press box for the playoffs, which becomes even bigger for the World Series.

"The days of the 70,000-seat stadiums are gone, so the teams really have to detail their plan," Capilli said.

For Division Series and League Championship Series games, MLB provides all teams with a range of ticket prices. The place where each team ranks on that scale depends on the size of the market and the costs of the regular-season tickets.

Major League Baseball, however, sets the prices for World Series games. By the time teams clinch World Series berths, clubs have long ago determined which seats will be available to the general public for purchase. Clubs aim to conduct the public sale shortly after securing a place in the Fall Classic to give fans as much time as possible to travel to the event. But even then, there isn't much time, especially if a League Championship Series extends to seven games.

The advent of online ticket sales means that fans are no longer forced to camp out overnight — or even for several days — waiting for tickets to be made available in a given location. In recent years, teams have implemented online lotteries in which fans enter their e-mail addresses on team websites to become eligible to purchase tickets. Winners can log on at appointed times, enter a password and then purchase a designated number of tickets, usually two to four per game.

Tickets that are purchased online can be printed from a home computer and feature barcodes that are scanned at the ballpark gate. The tickets sent to season-ticket holders and issued by MLB look much more traditional. They are produced from a template that's provided by Capilli's office and printed by the host teams with the help of two printing companies which are used by teams throughout baseball.

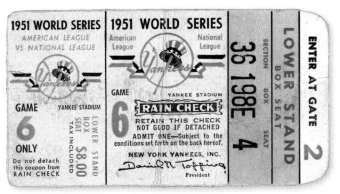

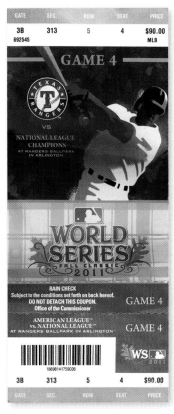

TIMES ARE CHANGING Major League Baseball works with teams to plan playoff ticket sales, and fans can now buy tickets in online lotteries.

FIRST PITCH

THE MOST DRAMATIC ceremonial first pitch in World Series history came on Oct. 30, 2001. Less than two months after the Sept. 11 terrorist attacks, President George W. Bush took the field at Yankee Stadium prior to Game 3 amid unprecedented security.

Unlike most ceremonial first pitchers, Bush stood atop the mound, not closer to the plate. That may have been prompted by some friendly ribbing from Yankees shortstop Derek Jeter, who warned: "This is New York. If you throw from the base of the mound, they're going to boo you."

President Bush was the first sitting president to deliver a World Series first pitch since Dwight D. Eisenhower in 1956. Wearing a bullet-proof vest under his jacket, he delivered a strike to Yankees backup catcher Todd Greene as chants of "U-S-A, U-S-A" rang out through the House That Ruth Built. Bush also threw out the first pitch before Game 4 of both the 2010 and 2011 World Series in Texas.

The process of choosing someone to throw a ceremonial pitch begins during the regular season. In mid-September, contending clubs prepare potential pitchers for MLB. The list often includes prominent local politicians and celebrities, former players and team owners, and retired baseball legends from the area. Former Cardinals greats, NBA star Dirk Nowitzki and Dallas Cowboys legend Roger Staubach were among those on the mound in 2011.

These days, the first pitch is really the second pitch. The actual first pitch, which is not filmed for television, is sometimes thrown by a representative of one of Major League Baseball's top sponsors or a winner of a sponsor sweepstakes. It's a low-key part of the ceremony, but one that has become quite important.

"Our goal is to give the fans and our various business partners access to the World Series in unique ways," said Tim Brosnan, MLB's executive vice president for business. "We want to accomplish that without causing a single bit of distraction to the two clubs that are competing."

Aside from the first pitches, pregame ceremonies also include the delivery of the game ball to the mound, which is often done by a local VIP. It could be someone affiliated with the host club, or someone who has made a great impact in the local community. For Game 3 of the 2008 World Series in Philadelphia, the Phillies and Major League Baseball invited country music star Tim McGraw as a symbolic gesture to honor his late father, Tug McGraw, who pitched the team to a World Series victory in 1980.

Unlike preparations for the national anthem, there's no on-field rehearsal for those tossing out the first pitch, although honorees can warm up in the batting cages beneath the stadium. It's not uncommon for fans to boo a poor throw, albeit in good nature.

"Many of the people chosen are former players, at least at some level," said Marla Miller, senior vice president for special events. "It's a tremendous honor that people seem to be well prepared for, especially at the World Series."

HONORED President George W. Bush threw out the ceremonial first pitch before Game 3 of the 2001 World Series at Yankee Stadium.

WALLS OF HISTORY The World Series Autumn Glory exhibit in Cooperstown grows each year.

HALL OF FAME

EACH YEAR, THE World Series features players who might one day be honored with an induction into the National Baseball Hall of Fame in Cooperstown, N.Y.

But each time a new champion is crowned, artifacts from the Fall Classic arrive within days to be displayed as part of the Autumn Glory exhibit, which features such historic items as the final-out ball from the 1903 World Series, the mitt that Yogi Berra wore to catch Don Larsen's perfect game in 1956, and the bat (which is now bronzed) that Bill Mazeroski used to hit his dramatic World Series–winning home run in 1960.

Much of the Autumn Glory exhibit is permanent, but one display case is dedicated to the most recent World Series. By mid-November, items from that year's World Series are on display, and artifacts from the previous Fall Classic are stored for future use.

Public relations officials from the Hall of Fame work during each Fall Classic to acquire donations from players and teams that best represent the event. During the World Series, the Hall officials on site keep in contact with curators in Cooperstown to determine which artifacts would best tell the story of that particular World Series.

"The players are incredibly generous, and we understand if they want to keep a particular item," said Craig Muder, director of communications for the Hall of Fame. "But usually they're receptive to the idea."

The Hall of Fame receives all types of different artifacts at the conclusion of the World Series, from bats — like the one that Philadelphia hurler Joe Blanton used to belt the first World Series home run by a pitcher in 34 years in 2008 — to balls, press pins, programs, photographs, spikes and helmets.

Such artifacts add to the Hall's legendary collection of World Series memorabilia that dates back to 1903, the year considered to be the start of the modern Fall Classic. But the Hall's treasure trove includes items representing every era, such as a bat used by outfielder Earle Combs in 1927 — when he was a member of the Yankees' Murderers' Row team, widely considered the greatest ballclub ever. That year, Combs scored six runs against the Pittsburgh Pirates in New York's sweep of the World Series. Also on display is the final-out ball from Game 1 that year, which was donated by Yankees legend Lou Gehrig and his wife before he passed away.

Although the National Baseball Hall of Fame has a collection of priceless pieces that are always available for the public to enjoy, the World Series additions are a hugely popular attraction in Cooperstown when they're unveiled each November, upon the conclusion of the baseball postseason.

"Fans are able to see these important artifacts from just days ago from an event they witnessed, at least on television," said Tom Shieber, the senior curator for the Hall of Fame's collections. "Right away, they can view them within the context of so many great moments in World Series history."

COMMISSIONER'S TROPHY

THE COMMISSIONER'S TROPHY — more commonly referred to as "The World Series Trophy" — was first awarded in 1967 when the St. Louis Cardinals defeated the Boston Red Sox. Unlike hockey's Stanley Cup, which is transferred from team to team each season, a new Commissioner's Trophy is created each year and presented to the winning team by the Commissioner of Major League Baseball at the conclusion of the World Series.

Originally designed by Lawrence Voegele of Owatonna, Minn., the trophy was redesigned slightly in 1999 by Tiffany & Co. Today's edition stands 24 inches tall, excluding the base, and measures 11 inches in diameter. Weighing 30 pounds, it is made of sterling silver and features 30 gold-plated, hand-furled flags — one for each Major League team — which rise above an arched silver baseball with latitude and longitude lines to symbolize the earth. The baseball itself weighs more than 10 pounds and features the Commissioner's signature. The previous design included pins at the base of the trophy representing the teams competing in the Fall Classic. The newer version, first presented to the New York Yankees following the 2000 World Series, has an estimated value of $15,000.

The Commissioner's Trophy, unlike the Stanley Cup, the Vince Lombardi Trophy (NFL) and the Larry O'Brien Trophy (NBA), is the only championship award of the four major U.S. sports not named after an individual. In 2008, MLB began showcasing the Commissioner's Trophy to the public prior to the World Series, placing it on display at city halls in Florida and Philadelphia. Ryan Wagner of the MLB Fan Cave took the trophy on a tour of postseason cities in October 2011.

"It's a great way for the fans to get ready and excited before the World Series," said Matt Bourne, MLB's vice president of business public relations.

PRIZED POSSESSION The official Major League Baseball World Series trophy is awarded each year. This one went to the White Sox in 2005.

WORLD SERIES RINGS

PLAYERS WHO WIN the World Series have to wait more than five months for the most tangible reward of their success. That's how long it takes for teams to design and produce the World Series rings. Given the size, detail and materials involved, it's no wonder it takes so long.

The Florida Marlins set a new standard for knuckle-busting jewelry with their 2003 model. With team owner and art dealer Jeffrey Loria overseeing the design, the Marlins' ring weighed in at 70 grams (three and a half ounces) and featured 228 diamonds, 13 rubies and a rare teal diamond for the eye of the Marlin.

"It's huge, a work of art," said Jeff Conine, the only member of the 2003 Marlins who also played on the club's '97 championship team. The following year, Boston was more conservative with their design, which featured a ruby "B" bedecked with 14 large diamonds and another five dozen smaller ones to add sparkle to the ring face.

It was the first Red Sox ring ever issued, as the team's previous titles came before bands were awarded. The 1922 Giants, who beat the Yankees, became the first team to get rings. At that time, World Series winners typically received watch fobs, medallions or other trinkets. Since 1931, all World Series champs have received rings.

The Red Sox issued a record 500 rings in 2004. Besides players and the coaching staff, much of the World Series–winning front office typically receives one. Owners also use rings to reward loyal friends and benefactors of the team, and players are offered the chance to purchase additional rings.

Rings are typically presented during a pregame ceremony early in the following season, and teams will often hand-deliver rings to players who moved to other clubs during the offseason after a win.

It's believed that the rings, designed in recent years by Jostens and InterGold, cost teams between $10,000 and $20,000 apiece, depending on the specifics of the design and the size of the order. With rings having become so large, players have been given the opportunity to purchase smaller, less expensive versions for everyday wear. Many players keep their rings in safes, taking them out for special occasions or to serve as motivation.

"I like bling as much as the next guy," said Cliff Floyd, a member of the 1997 world champion Marlins team. "But you're just not going to wear something like that on a regular basis."

Eric Hinske, who played for the world champion Red Sox in 2007 and the Rays in '08, was surprised when a few of his former Boston teammates showed up in Florida with a personal delivery in April 2008. As Hinske's young teammates passed the ring around, few could have imagined they'd be playing in the Fall Classic six months later.

"They all thought, 'Wouldn't it be awesome to have one of those?'" Hinske said. "It's what you play for, and nobody can ever take it away from you."

BUSCH STADIUM

DESPITE SHARING ITS name, Busch Stadium differs greatly from its forbearer. In 2006, the Cardinals left the cookie-cutter version for a state-of-the-art venue. The team immediately saw success, winning its 10th World Series in the park's inaugural season

Designed with scenery in mind, Busch Stadium provides a view of downtown St. Louis beyond the outfield, with the gateway Arch featuring prominently on the skyline. Various entrances are adorned with statues and other tokens from the old Busch Stadium, including a bronze statue of Stan Musial. In an average season, more than 3 million fans pass through Busch Stadium's gates.

Other aspects of the old park that got passed on include Big Mac Land and the sea of red seats. Unlike the former home, the new park has an open-air environment and large concourses from which fans can see the field.

In 2009, all eyes were on St. Louis when it hosted baseball's Midsummer Classic for the first time since 1966. The AL won, 4-3, to extend its unbeaten streak to 13 games.

In recent years, Busch Stadium has also established itself as a legitimate concert venue. In 2008, it hosted its first when the Dave Matthews Band played in front of 35,000 fans. Since then, the Eagles and U2 have also headlined shows played at Busch Stadium.

BIRTH OF THE CARDINALS

THE CARDINALS FRANCHISE has seemingly always enjoyed success, even dating back to its roots in the 1880s.

Founded as the St. Louis Brown Stockings, the Cards originally played in the American Association. The team played its games at several different venues known as Sportsman's Park from 1882–1892 and 1920–1966, with a stop in Robison Field along the way. It won plenty in Sportsman's Park, earning four pennants in a row from 1885–1888 and playing the Chicago White Stockings, who later became the Cubs, in an early version of the World Series — the beginning of the heated Cardinals-Cubs rivalry.

The American Association went bankrupt in 1892 but St. Louis's ballclub did not fade away, instead joining the National League. Although it took some time in the NL for the Cardinals to reach the same levels of earlier success, which they did behind Branch Rickey and the game's first Minor League system during the 1920s, the club found its identity after going through a pair of name changes. For 1899, the team adopted the name of the "Perfectos." The moniker died quickly, though, and just a year later the club became the Cardinals, which has remained the team name ever since.

THE ROSTER

THE 2011 ST. LOUIS CARDINALS

TONY LA RUSSA
MANAGER

IN COMPLETING HIS 16th season with the Cardinals, La Russa padded his franchise-leading victory total and surpassed 1,400 wins in St. Louis. His unconventional bullpen management paid off throughout the 2011 postseason; a previously maligned relief staff recorded more outs in the National League Championship Series against the Brewers than the St. Louis starters, as La Russa's mixing and matching paid off gloriously.

COACHING STAFF:
Dave Duncan: Pitching
Derek Lilliquist: Bullpen
Mark McGwire: Hitting
Dave McKay: First Base
Jose Oquendo: Third Base
Joe Pettini: Bench

10

LANCE BERKMAN
OUTFIELD

A 13-YEAR MAJOR League veteran, Lance Berkman experienced a career resurgence after joining St. Louis in the offseason. Getting off to a hot start in April — a month in which he had a trio of two-homer games and was twice named NL Player of the Week — the switch-hitting slugger returned to the offensive form that fans had come to expect from him in seasons past. At 35 years old, Berkman wasted no time settling into the heart of his new lineup and finished the regular season with a .301 batting average, a .412 on-base percentage and 31 homers.

12

MITCHELL BOGGS
PITCHER

DRAFTED BY THE Cardinals in 2005, Boggs made his Big League debut for the club three years later. Spending parts of the 2008 and '09 seasons in the Majors, the hard-throwing right-handed reliever pitched his first full campaign last year. In 2011, he appeared in relief 51 times, going two or more innings 10 times. Boggs also posted a career-low ERA and notched the first four saves of his career.

CHRIS CARPENTER
PITCHER

THE CARDINALS' NO. 1 starter this season, the 36-year-old Carpenter threw the second most innings of his career while facing a total of 996 batters in the 2011 regular season, a career high. A workhorse on the mound who features a five-pitch arsenal, Carpenter threw four complete games this season, two of which were shutouts, to propel the Redbirds into the playoffs — his fifth postseason appearance with the club. He added another shutout in Game 5 of the NLDS against Roy Halladay and the Phillies, cementing the Cardinals' spot in the NLCS.

29

ADRON CHAMBERS
OUTFIELD

A HOMEGROWN OUTFIELD prospect, Chambers was not called up from Triple-A Memphis until early September, but he showed enough promise for St. Louis to take him along for a postseason ride. After making his Major League debut on Sept. 6, the 25-year-old Chambers posted four RBI — three of which came on a pinch-hit, bases-clearing triple against the Mets on Sept. 20 — in just eight at-bats in the season's final month before adding another in the National League Division Series against the Phillies.

56

ALLEN CRAIG
UTILITY

ALTHOUGH A KNEE injury cost Craig the entire month of July, he made his presence known down the stretch once he returned. The versatile 27-year-old played six different defensive positions for the Redbirds this season, finishing the year with a .315 average, a .917 OPS and 11 home runs — five of which came in September — in 75 games. Craig also came up big in the playoffs, adding a triple in his first career postseason at-bat and collecting his first playoff home run in Game 4 of the NLCS. And in each of the first two World Series games, he came off the bench to face the Rangers' dominant pitcher Alexi Ogando, and both times cracked an RBI single to put the Cardinals ahead.

21

DANIEL DESCALSO
INFIELD

A ROOKIE WHO made his Major League debut with the Cardinals in September 2010, Descalso displayed his versatility during the 2011 campaign. Not only did the left-handed-hitting Descalso have a .278 average and a .434 on-base percentage with runners in scoring position this year while collecting several timely hits, but he also filled in at multiple key spots in the infield. The bulk of his time was spent at third, but Descalso, a California native and yet another of the Cards' homegrown prospects, also tried his hand at shortstop and second base.

33

OCTAVIO DOTEL
PITCHER

AFTER BEGINNING HIS Big League career and spending the better part of six seasons in the National League, Dotel played in the Junior Circuit for much of the next eight years. But he returned to his roots in the middle of this campaign — his 13th in The Show — after being traded to the Cardinals just before the July deadline. The right-handed reliever posted a paltry 0.85 WHIP in 24.2 innings with his new club. And few were better than the veteran at suppressing right-handed batters, as he excelled throughout his first trip to the postseason.

28

DAVID FREESE
THIRD BASE

FREESE HARDLY REGISTERED on the national scene before the 2011 postseason, but he enjoyed quite the coming-out party in the NLCS. Rebounding from a hand injury that kept him out of the lineup for all of May and most of June, Freese, in his second full Big League campaign, hit .297 with a .350 on-base percentage and 10 homers. But once the October stage was set, Freese handled himself with the poise of a veteran, racking up five hits — including one home run — in the NLDS while adding another 12 base knocks and three long-balls in NLCS play.

23

RAFAEL FURCAL
SHORTSTOP

COMING OVER FROM the Dodgers in a trade-deadline deal, Furcal took over as the Cardinals' everyday shortstop, boasting one of the strongest arms of any infielder in the Major Leagues. The career National Leaguer appeared in 50 games for the Redbirds, also assuming responsibility as their leadoff hitter. A seasoned veteran in the playoffs despite never having played in the World Series before this year, Furcal amassed eight hits in the first nine games of the 2011 postseason, coming around to score for St. Louis five times in that span.

JAIME GARCIA
PITCHER

BUMPED UP TO the No. 2 spot in the Cardinals' rotation following Adam Wainwright's season-ending injury during Spring Training, Garcia followed his stellar rookie showing with a campaign that showed no signs of a sophomore slump. On April 3, in his first start of the year, the Mexico native tossed a complete-game shutout — the first of the year in the Majors — and added another before season's end. Matching his victories total from 2010 with 13, Garcia managed to cut down on walks allowed. The left-hander also showed some prowess at the plate, as he launched his first career home run against the Milwaukee Brewers — the team he and the Cardinals would later meet in the NLCS — on Aug. 2.

TYLER GREENE
INFIELD

A 28-YEAR-OLD INFIELDER out of Georgia Tech, Greene spent much of the early season with the club before alternating between St. Louis and its Triple-A affiliate in Memphis. But Greene was called up in September to help the Cardinals in their playoff push, and he proved adept, getting on base at a .419 clip with runners in scoring position. He was especially effective hitting on the road, where his OPS was more than 200 points higher than at home.

27

MATT HOLLIDAY
OUTFIELD

WHEN HOLLIDAY WAS acquired from the Oakland Athletics at the July trade deadline in 2009, he was brought in to provide a bat to complement Albert Pujols' in the St. Louis lineup. Holliday has done that and more, as he was an All-Star for the second time as a member of the Cardinals in 2011. Holliday has averaged 42 doubles and 28 home runs over the past six seasons, and he overcame hand injuries this year to hit .435 in the National League Championship Series against the Brewers.

The Cardinals locked Holliday up to a seven-year deal early in the 2010 season, and he has already rewarded the franchise with 50 home runs and 81 doubles to go along with a .305 batting average in his two full seasons in St. Louis, filling the exact role the Cardinals brought him in for.

7

EDWIN JACKSON
PITCHER

ALTHOUGH JUST 28 years of age, Jackson is no stranger to relocation. He was traded for the sixth time in his career when St. Louis acquired him in the middle of the season. Jackson was stingy, yielding three or fewer earned runs in 10 of his 12 starts for the Cardinals. In the post-season, he delivered his biggest start as a Redbird by pitching six frames of two-run ball against the Phillies in the Division Series. St. Louis would go on to a 5-3 win and would stave off elimination thanks to the effort.

22

JON JAY
OUTFIELD

PATROLLING THE OUTFIELD in between Matt Holliday and Lance Berkman, the 26-year-old Jay had a productive first full season with the Cardinals, both offensively and defensively. In a lineup stacked with solid offensive contributors, Jay made a habit of punishing pitchers early in the count, hitting .464 on first-pitch balls put into play. Taking over for Colby Rasmus, who was dealt to the Blue Jays during the season, Jay made just three errors against five assists in the outfield in 2011.

19

GERALD LAIRD
CATCHER

AFTER EIGHT SEASONS serving as a catcher for the Texas Rangers and then the Detroit Tigers, Laird made his first World Series during his debut season with the Cardinals, a year that saw him serve as a reliable backup to Yadier Molina. The former second-round pick of the Oakland Athletics had his best year at the plate in 2006, when he hit .296 with a .332 OBP and an .805 OPS in 78 games.

13

KYLE LOHSE
PITCHER

IN HIS FOURTH season with the Cardinals, Lohse posted a career-best ERA (3.39) while more than doubling his 2010 innings. Putting an injury-marred 2010 behind him, Lohse's contributions helped solidify a Cardinals staff that needed to fill the void left by Adam Wainwright's Spring Training injury. From July 24 through season's end, he went on a run of 10 starts in which he allowed three earned runs or fewer.

26

LANCE LYNN
PITCHER

LYNN WAS REGARDED as an early-season favorite to take the injured Adam Wainwright's rotation spot, but instead he spent the first two months of the season in Triple-A to fine tune his repertoire. Upon his June call-up to St. Louis, Lynn proved to be a strikeout force in his rookie season, whiffing 40 batters and walking just 11 in 34.2 innings pitched across two starts and 16 relief appearances.

62

KYLE McCLELLAN
PITCHER

McCLELLAN GOT PLENTY of work early in the season as the Cardinals' No. 5 starter. Joining the rotation for the first time in his career, the righty crafted a 6-2 record while posting a 3.18 ERA in his first nine Big League starts. Later in the season, after the arrival of Edwin Jackson, McClellan saw time out of the bullpen, thriving in August when he picked up another three victories and recorded a paltry 1.06 ERA in 17 innings of relief.

46

YADIER MOLINA
CATCHER

ONE OF THE Majors' best defensive catchers, Molina has thrown out an impressive 44 percent of attempted base stealers in his career to date. His defense has always been a known commodity, but the 2011 season also saw a breakout offensive campaign for the 29-year-old Puerto Rico native. Setting career highs in numerous major statistical categories — including home runs, doubles, runs scored and RBI — Molina helped power a Cardinals offense that led the NL in runs scored, batting average and on-base percentage.

The youngest of the three catching Molina brothers carried a .305 average into the post-season and then went on to collect eight hits against the Brewers in the NLCS.

JASON MOTTE
PITCHER

MOTTE THRIVES IN the late innings of ballgames, and although he was never officially dubbed the Cardinals' closer this season — at least not publicly — the 29-year-old fireballer saw most of his work come in the eighth and ninth frames. In 68 innings pitched in 2011, Motte struck out 63 and posted a career-low 0.956 WHIP. And when the Cards found themselves battling for a playoff spot, it was Motte who contributed an ERA lower than 2.00 in 11 September games, going 8 for 9 in save chances.

30

COREY PATTERSON
OUTFIELD

ACQUIRED AS PART of the big deal that sent young center fielder Colby Rasmus north of the border to the Toronto Blue Jays, Patterson provided versatility at all three outfield spots for the Cardinals. In more than 750 innings in the outfield this season with both the Cards and Blue Jays, Patterson committed just one error and recorded four assists, providing late-inning defensive insurance that Manager Tony La Russa utilized with regularity toward the end of the year.

44

ALBERT PUJOLS
FIRST BASE

A SLOW START this season, followed by a fractured wrist in June, had some forecasting trouble for the Majors' predominant slugger. Pujols isn't one to bow to skeptics, but he proved his doubters wrong by making his way back to the lineup less than three weeks after the injury and returning to his old self. The 31-year-old picked up his production in the second half and went on a tear as the Cardinals edged into the postseason, getting on base at a .393 clip and contributing 38 hits in September. Once in the World Series, he put on a power display, launching three mammoth homers in Game 3.

5

NICK PUNTO
SECOND BASE

BACK IN THE National League for the first time since 2003, Punto provided valuable defensive versatility in the infield. the nine-year veteran made the most of his opportunities for playing time with the Cardinals, as his .388 on-base percentage — a career high — makes apparent. A regular starter in the past as a member of the Twins, the 33-year-old dutifully filled his diminished role, enjoying success in his first opportunity to face National League pitching since manning the middle infield with Philadelphia.

8

ARTHUR RHODES
PITCHER

THE CARDINALS BECAME the ninth Major League team to employ Rhodes when they acquired him in mid-August following his release from the Cardinals' World Series opponent, the Texas Rangers. Rhodes had seen his strikeout numbers slip and his ERA rise while with the Rangers, but after the move he found National League lefties to be a bit more to his liking. The 42-year-old Rhodes has been a beast against left-handed batters throughout his 20-year career, holding them to a .611 OPS, and Rhodes was able to provide similar production for a Cardinals team that gave him a second chance during the '11 season.

53

MARC RZEPCZYNSKI
PITCHER

DON'T LET THE 3.97 ERA fool you: Rzepczynski was just as effective in his stint with the Cardinals as he was with the Blue Jays in 2011. The Toronto import saw his strikeout rate skyrocket to more than 11 per nine innings on average upon moving to the NL, and that swing-and-miss stuff continued to flourish in the postseason. In his first taste of playoff action after being traded, Rzepczynski struck out five of the first 23 batters he faced, permitting just five hits. Only one of those came off the bat of a Milwaukee Brewer, as Rzepczynski permitted just two base runners in 4.2 innings in the NLCS.

34

FERNANDO SALAS
PITCHER

SALAS PAID NO mind to whether a lefty or righty was batting, as he held both to an OPS lower than .650 in 2011. He filled every role in the bullpen: middle relief, situational, set-up and closing, and he performed admirably in each. Salas was the go-to ninth-inning arm early in the season, posting a 1.88 ERA and going 8 for 8 in save chances in May; he would finish the season as the Cardinals' leader in saves with 24. Perhaps Salas's biggest appearance came in Game 2 of the LDS, when he stymied the Philadelphia Phillies in the fourth and fifth innings as the St. Louis offense mounted a comeback against Cliff Lee.

59

EDUARDO SANCHEZ
PITCHER

SANCHEZ, A 22-YEAR-OLD rookie from Venezuela, made his Major League debut in mid-April against the Arizona Diamondbacks, and it was one that certainly piqued the interest of Cards fans looking for bullpen depth. Sanchez tossed two scoreless innings of one-hit relief, striking out five of the seven batters he faced that day. This was no fluke, either, as Sanchez struck out nearly half of all the batters he went up against in April; 17 of 36 in 10 innings, to be precise. With a mid-90s fastball and a hard curveball, it's easy to see why Sanchez generated as many K's as he did early in the season.

52

SKIP SCHUMAKER
UTILITY

ALTHOUGH AN INJURY sidelined him for the NLCS, Schumaker was elemental in getting the Cardinals to the next round in the first place. His double in the first inning of Game 5 of the Division Series scored the game's first and only run as starter Chris Carpenter made Schumaker's effort last the remainder of the game. The career Cardinal hit a solid .283 in 400 plate appearances during the regular season while playing a steady second base.

55

RYAN THERIOT
INFIELD

AFTER NEARLY FIVE seasons with the division-rival Cubs, Theriot was brought in by St. Louis following the 2010 season for his gritty play and middle-infield defense. Filling the void left when Brendan Ryan was traded to Seattle before the 2011 season, the Louisiana native spent most of his time at shortstop, but also contributed 17 starts at second base. Playing in the bright lights of the postseason for the first time since an '08 trip with the Cubs, Theriot's shining moments came in Games 2 and 3 of the Division Series against Philadelphia. He collected six hits in two games; one scored the first run in a comeback effort against Cliff Lee and four came in a close Game 3 loss.

3

JAKE WESTBROOK
PITCHER

ACQUIRED IN 2010 as part of a shake-up that involved shipping out outfielder Ryan Ludwick, Westbrook's first full season in the National League yielded his most victories since 2006. After he was re-signed by the Cards prior to the 2011 campaign, he returned to the postseason for the first time since 2007, when his Cleveland Indians succumbed to the Boston Red Sox in the ALCS. Westbrook was one of four pitchers on the staff with 100-plus strikeouts, and his durability was evident: His 33 starts ranked second behind only Chris Carpenter. Westbrook even flashed some power with the bat, swatting his first career home run — a grand slam, no less — against the Brewers in late August.

35

2011 SEASON IN REVIEW

THE TONE FOR the 2011 season was set before the year had even begun, when the Phillies signed lefty Cliff Lee in December 2010. It looked like their rotation had entered another stratosphere and, as evidenced by dynamic pitching performances throughout the season, nothing is more important than elite hurlers. Across the Bigs, arms stole headlines. Justin Verlander was nearly unbeatable, while Clayton Kershaw became the most overpowering pitcher in the National league, winning the pitching version of the triple crown.

As the calendar neared October, fans were treated to some unexpected playoff races, as both the Cardinals and Rays made historic comebacks on their way to tying up the NL and AL Wild Card races, respectively, as they headed into the season's final game. And what a day that was. With arguably the most thrilling finale to a season ever, baseball again proved that nothing is over until the final out.

BEST OF 2011

AMAZING ARMS

WITH OFFENSE IN the Bigs reaching a two-decade low in 2011 — teams averaged 4.28 runs per game, the lowest since 1992, when they averaged 4.12 — plenty of pitchers shined, but among those, a few stood apart from the pack.

No player owned 2011 like Justin Verlander. With the combination of a blazing fastball and knee-buckling curveball, Verlander baffled opponents, striking out 250 hitters and limiting them to a sub-Mendoza line batting average. His highlight came when he threw his second career no-hitter, against Toronto in May. This nasty stuff propelled the right-hander to 24 wins, including 12 straight down the stretch as the Tigers rolled into the playoffs.

While Verlander was by far the most talented starter on the Tigers, Cliff Lee managed to stand out among a horde of aces. Lee more than lived up to expectations in his first year back in Philly. The lefty struck out hitters at a career-high rate, punching out more than one per inning.

On the West Coast, 23-year-old **Clayton Kershaw** established himself among baseball's elite, winning the pitching version of the NL triple crown with 21 victories, a 2.28 ERA and 248 K's.

And up the highway just a bit, Jered Weaver broke out of the gates with a 6-0 record in April that included a 15-strikeout manhandling of the Blue Jays and an ERA below 1.00. Weaver set the tone for an incredible first half that earned him the start in the All-Star Game. He emerged as one of baseball's best pitchers this season and kept the Angels in the playoff hunt.

FINAL STANDINGS

AMERICAN LEAGUE

East	W	L	GB
xNew York	97	65	-
yTampa Bay	91	71	6
Boston	90	72	7
Toronto	81	81	16
Baltimore	69	93	28

Central	W	L	GB
xDetroit	95	67	-
Cleveland	80	82	15
Chicago	79	83	16
Kansas City	71	91	24
Minnesota	63	99	32

West	W	L	GB
xTexas	96	66	-
Los Angeles	86	76	10
Oakland	74	88	22
Seattle	67	95	29

NATIONAL LEAGUE

East	W	L	GB
xPhiladelphia	102	60	-
Atlanta	89	73	13
Washington	80	81	21.5
New York	77	85	25
Florida	72	90	30

Central	W	L	GB
xMilwaukee	96	66	-
ySt. Louis	90	72	6
Cincinnati	79	83	17
Pittsburgh	72	90	24
Chicago	71	91	25
Houston	56	106	40

West	W	L	GB
xArizona	94	68	-
San Francisco	86	76	8
Los Angeles	82	79	11.5
Colorado	73	89	21
San Diego	71	91	23

x Division winner; y Wild Card

2011 CATEGORY LEADERS

AMERICAN LEAGUE

Batting Average	Miguel Cabrera, Detroit	.344
Hits	Michael Young, Texas	213
	Adrian Gonzalez, Boston	
Home Runs	Jose Bautista, Toronto	43
RBI	Curtis Granderson, New York	119
Stolen Bases	Coco Crisp, Oakland	49
	Brett Gardner, New York	
Wins	Justin Verlander, Detroit	24
ERA	Justin Verlander, Detroit	2.40
Strikeouts	Justin Verlander, Detroit	250
Saves	Jose Valverde, Detroit	49

NATIONAL LEAGUE

Batting Average	Jose Reyes, New York	.337
Hits	Starlin Castro, Chicago	207
Home Runs	Matt Kemp, Los Angeles	39
RBI	Matt Kemp, Los Angeles	126
Stolen Bases	Michael Bourn, Atlanta	61
Wins	Ian Kennedy, Arizona	21
	Clayton Kershaw, Los Angeles	
ERA	Clayton Kershaw, Los Angeles	2.28
Strikeouts	Clayton Kershaw, Los Angeles	248
Saves	John Axford, Milwaukee	46
	Craig Kimbrel, Atlanta	

APRIL 2011

DEEP SEA PITCHING

Few pitchers have better pure stuff than righty **Josh Johnson** of the Florida Marlins, and he made that obvious in April. After flirting with multiple no-hitters early on — his best effort was limiting the Braves to one hit in 7.1 innings — Johnson recorded a 1.64 ERA in his first nine starts with a WHIP below 1.00.

JOEY BATS

Jose Bautista kicked off 2011 by blasting a home run on Opening Day, one of nine he would hit that month. He led the Major Leagues in bombs for a second straight year, which helped to silence those who questioned the validity of his breakout 2010 campaign. Even more impressively, Bautista actually improved on that 54-homer season by raising his batting average and showing improved discipline at the plate, asserting himself as one of baseball's most dangerous hitters.

THE CARDINALS ESTABLISHED themselves as a force early in the 2011 season, with a roster that included 19 players who were returning from 2010. One of those holdovers, starting pitcher **Jaime Garcia**, quickly asserted himself as a force to be reckoned with on the mound during his sophomore season in St. Louis. The southpaw threw the Majors' first shutout of the year — a 2-0 victory over the Padres on April 3 — on the road to his second straight 13-win campaign.

A newcomer to the club, Lance Berkman made his transition look seamless, blasting his first two longballs in a St. Louis uniform on April 11 against the Arizona Dia-mondbacks before also going on to homer in his next two games. The 35-year-old switch-hitting slugger finished the month with a trio of two–home run outings and a .393 batting average, twice claiming NL Player of the Week honors for his performance.

These hot starts helped the Cardinals come out on top in 16 of their first 27 April contests, including taking three of four from the Los Angeles Dodgers in the middle of the month. The club entered May leading the National League in batting average (.295) and runs scored (144) thanks in part to a seven-game streak in April during which the lineup piled up 106 base hits.

MAY 2011

EFFECTIVELY WILD

In one of the strangest no-hitters ever, **Francisco Liriano** walked six White Sox and struck out just two, but every ball in play found a fielder as the Pale Hose were unable to capitalize on Liriano's shaky control. Although the free passes threatened to turn Liriano into a pumpkin at any moment, the lefty persevered to make history on May 3.

ANDRE THE GIANT

Outfielder **Andre Ethier** has developed a reputation in Los Angeles as one of the Dodgers' most reliable bats. Ethier made his reputation national when he strung together a 30-game hitting streak, which stole the show for the first month and a half of the season. Ethier hit a remarkable .397 during the streak — which ended May 7 — and recorded 10 doubles, complementing a strong season from teammate and NL MVP candidate Matt Kemp.

FREAK SHOW

Following the Giants' first World Series championship in San Francisco in 2010, **Tim Lincecum** appeared determined to grab another. This was never more evident than in his May 21 start against the Oakland A's, when he retired 21 straight en route to a three-hit shutout. That was just one night in another typically dominant Lincecum season, which saw the right-hander hold hitters to a batting average below .220.

AFTER ENDURING TWO injury-marred seasons, Kyle Lohse found himself back at full strength and slotted into the No. 3 spot in the Cards' rotation. Despite dropping his first start, the right-hander bounced back to notch victories in each of his next four outings in April and added three more wins in May, finding himself deadlocked for the National League lead in wins with seven by the end of the month. Lohse also ranked third in ERA by that time, on his way to posting a career-best 3.39 mark for the season.

Another pleasant surprise for St. Louis was Kyle McClellan. Working in relief the previous three seasons, McClellan found himself a member of the Redbirds' rotation on Opening Day. The then-26-year-old righty seemed at ease in his new role, going 6-2 in his first 10 starts. McClellan posted a 3.86 ERA during his first two months as a starter before rejoining the bullpen in August once the club acquired Edwin Jackson via trade.

Rookie **Fernando Salas** showed versatility this season, as well. Despite having appeared out of the bullpen in 27 games last season, Salas got just one save opportunity. But in May, the young righty became the Cardinals' go-to ninth-inning arm, going 8 for 8 in save chances while posting a 1.88 ERA for the month. He would end the season as the team leader in saves with 24 before becoming a valuable set-up man in October.

JUNE 2011

AND MANY MORE ...

On June 30, New York Yankees first baseman **Mark Teixeira** hit his 300th career home run. The milestone blast came at home against the Brewers. Tex became the seventh switch-hitter to reach the mark, joining the likes of Mickey Mantle, Eddie Murray and Chipper Jones.

COMPLETE-GAME JAMES

After completing a total of five games in his first five years in the Bigs, **James Shields** made going the distance look simple in 2011. Highlighted by three straight complete games in June, Shields finished 11 starts this season to lead the Majors. In fact, no pitcher had reached double digits since Randy Johnson threw 12 complete games in 1999.

In an era when relief pitching is emphasized and starters rarely pitch deep into contests, Shields helped the Rays reach the postseason by becoming one of baseball's pre-eminent workhorses.

BUCKING THE TREND

When **Andrew McCutchen**'s 12th-inning blast gave the Pirates a 3-2 win over Arizona on June 8, it was the first time in nearly six years the club sat at .500 that late in the season. More importantly, the Pirates had momentum on the way to claiming first place in July for the first time since 1997. With a nucleus headlined by McCutchen, there is hope in Pittsburgh that better times are on the way.

NOT AN OVERWHELMING favorite before the season to take the NL Central crown, the Cardinals had their own ideas. The club had a 2.5-game lead in the standings when June began, but three weeks later, on June 19, the Cards suffered a frightening blow when first baseman **Albert Pujols** fractured his left wrist trying to make a tag in a game against Kansas City. Projected to miss six weeks, the three-time MVP was going to be impossible to replace. As tough a player as there is in the Bigs, the masher was activated from the DL just two weeks later, and the results from his second half speak for themselves.

Even with the loss of Pujols, the Baltimore Orioles found themselves at the mercy of the Cardinals' offense during June's Interleague Play. St. Louis took three consecutive games from Baltimore during their stint against clubs from the American League East. The third victory, a 9-6 triumph, put the Cardinals at 44-38 on the season and tied them for first place in the National League Central standings. Earlier in the month, it was the rival Chicago Cubs who fell victim to the Cardinals in a three-game set in the shadow of the Gateway Arch. Starter Jaime Garcia was the winning pitcher once in each series.

JULY 2011

3,000 IN STYLE

With all of the national attention on **Derek Jeter** and his pursuit of 3,000 hits, the Yankees' captain could not have found a more dramatic way to reach the milestone. Facing tough Rays lefty David Price, Jeter crushed a fastball to the left-field seats for his 3,000th hit, part of a 5-for-5 day. Jeter became just the second member of the 3,000-hit club to reach the mark on a home run, after Wade Boggs did so in 1999.

ERVIN LEGEND

For most of the season, the Angels were known for their rotation, led by Jered Weaver and Dan Haren. Fellow starter **Ervin Santana** forced his way into the conversation on July 27, when he threw a no-hitter against the Indians. After giving up an early, unearned run, Santana was untouchable, striking out 10 and allowing just one more base runner.

AS THE SEASON progressed, **Lance Berkman** proved to be just the offensive boost that the Cardinals' lineup needed. Berkman let his bat do the talking as he led the Senior Circuit in home runs for much of July before finishing the month with eight.

Thanks to his scorching first half of the season, Berkman would join his teammate and fellow outfielder Matt Holliday in Arizona after they were voted starters for the National League All-Star team on the fan ballot — their sixth and fifth Midsummer Classic nods, respectively — while catcher Yadier Molina, getting his third call, was among the reserves. Holliday also took part in the State Farm Home Run Derby during All-Star Week, sending five longballs over the fences at Chase Field.

The July excitement didn't end there; trades were the news of the summer for the Cardinals. Amid all the hype, the Redbirds managed to make some moves, picking up significant reinforcements when they acquired starting pitcher Edwin Jackson, bullpen arms Octavio Dotel and Marc Rzepczynski and outfielder Corey Patterson from the Blue Jays four days before the July 31 deadline in one of the year's biggest deals. The Cardinals made another key pickup on deadline day when they made a deal to obtain Rafael Furcal from the Dodgers.

AUGUST 2011

BRAVE NEW ROOKIE

A lack of experience did not hinder Braves rookie **Craig Kimbrel**, whose incendiary fastball helped him break baseball's rookie saves record of 41. After tying the mark on the final day of August, Kimbrel started September with a bang, striking out three Nationals to claim the record for his own.

GENTLEMAN JIM

Jim Thome may never have been the flashiest player, but he has lit up the scoreboard for the better part of two decades. On Aug. 15, Thome hit his 600th career home run, becoming the first to do so in the at-bat immediately after his 599th. Thome, who has had 17 seasons with 20-plus home runs, became just the eighth player in baseball history to reach the prodigious milestone.

STILL VERY MUCH in contention as the calendar turned from July to August, the Cardinals gained steam in a four-game series against the Florida Marlins. St. Louis swept the Fish during the roadtrip, scoring a combined 20 runs during that stretch. Unfortunately, that series would be followed by a run of 10 losses in 15 games that threatened to take the Cards out of the running. But in the month's final series, the Redbirds took three games from the division-rival Milwaukee Brewers — giving them another multi-sweep month, with both coming on the road — to finish August on the upswing. St. Louis scored 18 times during the latter series.

One of the team's hottest bats during the month belonged to Yadier Molina, the 29-year-old catcher who was in the midst of his eighth season with the Cardinals. Coming off his third-straight All-Star selection, the backstop proved his mettle at the plate, knocking 25 hits — including four that left the ballpark — in 21 games for the month while posting a .342 batting average and a .360 on-base percentage.

On the pitching side, **Kyle McClellan** adapted to whatever skipper Tony La Russa asked of him. Returning to the 'pen after working 17 games as a starter, he went 3-0 with a paltry 1.06 ERA in 17 innings of relief.

SEPTEMBER 2011

Peerless

At this point in **Mariano Rivera**'s illustrious career, it almost goes without saying that he is the best closer in the history of baseball. Between his regular-season and postseason dominance, Rivera's accomplishments are unmatched. Now, he has the record every closer seeks. On Sept. 19, Rivera passed Trevor Hoffman for the all-time saves mark, picking up his 602nd with a scoreless ninth against the Twins and adding another achievement to a career that will almost certainly end with an entry into Cooperstown.

Tremendous 20

Coming into the season, not many would have expected **Ian Kennedy** to be a Cy Young Award candidate. But when he picked up his 20th victory on Sept. 19, he definitively joined the discussion. With fellow emerging starter Daniel Hudson, closer J.J. Putz and a reinvented pitching staff, Kennedy and the D-backs clinched their first division title since 2007.

SEPTEMBER SAW A collective effort from Cardinals players to return to the postseason after a hiatus in 2010. After the games of Sept. 1, the club trailed the Brewers by 7.5 games in the NL Central and were 8.5 behind the Braves for the Wild Card spot. But 18 wins for the month — highlighted by a sweep of Atlanta — gave the Cardinals the advantage they needed.

Many heroes emerged during the stretch run, including Allen Craig, who spent much of the summer as a bench player. With the Cardinals back 8.5 games and making a push for the playoffs as autumn set in, the right-handed sophomore — who had proved his versatility by playing six different defensive positions throughout the year — went on a tear in the final month, batting .327 and getting on base at a .364 clip. He also contributed five home runs and 12 RBI in 20 games.

The usual suspects contributed, as well. Despite getting off to a slow start, Albert Pujols came back from his injury to post a red-hot second half that was highlighted by a .355 average in September — arguably his best month. His five home runs pushed him over the 35-homer threshold for the fourth straight year.

A bullpen shuffle also propelled the team to October. Taking over closing duties as the season wound down, reliever **Jason Motte** did not wilt under the pressure. The 29-year-old flame thrower kept his ERA well below 2.00 for most of the month, and he finished it 8 for 9 in save opportunities.

WILD WEDNESDAY

AFTER 140 GAMES, the playoff picture seemed fully developed. Somehow, though, after 161, it was anything but. Despite trailing the Red Sox by nine games going into the season's final month, the Tampa Bay Rays had stormed back in historic fashion to tie Boston for the AL Wild Card lead entering the final day of the regular season. And in the National League, the St. Louis Cardinals managed to come from behind to tie the Atlanta Braves for that circuit's Wild Card bid on the second-to-last day after being back 8.5 games going into September. What followed would be arguably the most exciting day of baseball in the history of the sport.

"Tonight was great for the game of baseball," MLB Network's Greg Amsinger would say on *MLB Tonight* following the games. "Write down the date — Sept. 28, 2011 — and remember it. Remember where you were. Try to think if you've ever lived through a better night of baseball."

With each consequential game — Braves-Phillies, Red Sox–Orioles, Cardinals-Astros and Rays-Yankees — happening at the same time, fans couldn't put the remote down, constantly switching around as one dramatic moment followed another.

The Cardinals' game finished first, with St. Louis ace Chris Carpenter calmly dissecting the Astros to the tune of 11 strikeouts, two hits and one walk in a shutout. With that, the Braves were on the ropes, needing a win to force a one-game playoff. With a 3-2 lead heading into the ninth, Atlanta appeared to be on its way to a one-game playoff, but rookie closer Craig Kimbrel couldn't shut the door, giving up a sac fly after loading the bases.

The score remained knotted at three heading into the 13th, when Hunter Pence put the Phillies ahead with a broken-bat single. A double play off the bat of Braves rookie Freddie Freeman in the bottom half of the inning ended Atlanta's season, officially cementing the Cards' comeback as the biggest September deficit ever erased — a mark that would stand for less than an hour.

In the AL, the Rays looked all but buried against the Yanks, falling behind, 7-0. But six runs in the eighth and a homer in the ninth would send the game to extra innings.

Meanwhile, the Red Sox went into the bottom of the ninth against the Orioles leading, 3-2. With two outs, Sox closer Jon Papelbon gave up back-to-back doubles to tie the game. The next hitter, Robert Andino, hit a sinking liner to left field that just got under Carl Crawford's glove, scoring the walk-off run. The last-place O's relished playing the role of spoiler, dogpiling on the mound as if they had just won a playoff berth themselves.

No more than five minutes later, back in Florida, the Rays' Evan Longoria made history twice with one swing, homering in the 12th on a rocket to left field to put the Rays in the playoffs with an 8-7 win. It broke the record set an hour earlier by the Cardinals for biggest comeback in September and also made Longoria the second player — the Giants' Bobby Thomson in 1951 was the other — ever to send his team to the postseason with a home run on the final day of the regular season.

"You couldn't script this," said MLB Network analyst Dan Plesac. "You know what's fair, though? Both winners of the Wild Card were playing better than anybody fighting for it. Not even close."

Robert Andino (opposite, top) spoiled Boston's hopes; Chris Carpenter and Yadier Molina (opposite, bottom) celebrated; and Evan Longoria's homer sent the Rays to the playoffs. Insets: MLB Network's Harold Reynolds (left) and Dan Plesac reacted to the action with awe.

ABOVE AND BEYOND

From his natural ability to his work ethic and toughness, nobody in baseball comes close to matching Albert Pujols.

By Jeff Passan

EVERY TIME ALBERT Pujols steps into the batter's box, he holds rapt an entire ballpark. Fans peer from luxury boxes and upper-deck seats located in another zip code hoping to witness greatness. Beer vendors make sure to walk down a staircase so as not to disrespect the moment by turning their backs. Ushers leave their posts. Groundskeepers disregard their dirt. The rest of the St. Louis Cardinals turn into an admiration society at the sheer hypnosis of the moment: Pujols waggling his bat, his people turning to putty at the possibility of what might happen.

The worst place to be at this moment isn't where you might think. Pitchers have this thing about facing Pujols, almost an air of resignation, and so the collective might of his skills neither frustrates nor intimidates them. It's a matter of when he'll get you, not if, so they just hope nobody's on base when inevitability strikes. It's like a prank: As long as it doesn't happen to you, it's great to see.

Except when you're crouching behind the plate, inches from Pujols and assigned the task of trying to beat him. Whereas the pitcher-versus-hitter battle has more to do with physical talent than anything, the catcher-versus-hitter face-off is entirely mental, a guessing game. What pitch does the hitter like? What is he looking for? Where should we throw it? How can we confuse him? The catcher and hitter engage in a psychological war without ever locking eyes, and it's one the catcher should win, because he gets to dictate where every pitch goes.

Unless the game is rigged, of course. See, Pujols doesn't really have a weakness of which to speak. Up and in, low and away, middle-in; the Cardinals' first baseman blankets the nine areas of the strike zone and turns catchers into basket cases. For more than a decade now, they have been trying to crack him, trying to find something that shows Pujols isn't baseball's HAL 9000, and at every turn they have failed. They keep coming back for more only because they have to.

"There are only a few guys I've ever caught where I'm behind the plate and have no idea what to call," says Dodgers catcher Rod Barajas. "Because he can hit this, hit that, hit this, hit that. You're just hoping that, for some reason, he's off just a little bit, gets under the ball and hits it to the warning track."

That is what it has come to: A near–home run is seen as the best-case scenario. The level of reverence for Albert Pujols, baseball player, is unmatched among his peers and unseen in the game for decades. Fans and players alike admire Derek Jeter for his class, and they venerated Barry Bonds for his bat, and they turned Pedro Martinez and Greg Maddux into deities during their primes. Not since perhaps Hank Aaron, though, has a player been so simultaneously feared and respected as Pujols.

Never mind that Pujols is, by both friends' and foes' accounts, a wonderful man who donates much time and money to charity and has woven himself into the tapestry of St. Louis since joining the Cards in 2001. Disregard that he has stayed out of trouble, too. Because the admiration is purely professional, and it goes back to three traits that continue to define him.

CONSISTENCY IS THE easiest to understand since it's so obvious. It's not just that Pujols may have had the best 10-year stretch ever to start a career, that he hit more homers and doubles over that span than anyone in the NL. It's that every single year he puts up mind-boggling numbers. He rarely has an off-day, let alone an off-week, month or, laughably, year.

"He's just so consistent," the Braves' Jason Heyward says. "In everything. More times than not, he's successful because he can repeat it. He uses what he has, and he uses it so well. I love watching him hit. The way he's able to keep his bat head level — it stays in the zone for so long. Anyone would love to have his approach."

Of all his qualities, it's perhaps his consistency that Pujols cherishes most. When the Cards chose him with the 402nd pick in the 1999 draft, they worried most about reliability. Cardinals GM John Mozeliak, then the club's scouting director, knew the talent within Pujols. Nurturing it daily, though, and ensuring that it didn't lapse, would be the difficult part. After originally offering him $10,000 to sign, the Cardinals met his $60,000 asking price and figured it a worthwhile gamble.

Any concerns about consistency vanished during his lone Minor League season in 2000, when he leapt from Class-A to Triple-A at just 20 years of age. He arrived in The Show the next year and hit .329 with 37 home runs and 130 RBI. His career averages: .328 with 40 home runs and 121 RBI per season.

"There have been guys that have had years as good, but nobody has had as many good years as Albert has," says teammate Lance Berkman, who, for a decade, faced Pujols as a member of the Houston Astros. "He does it year in and year out. It's like clockwork. There aren't many guys who average 40 homers a year. He's one. And you know where it starts?

"Albert's very focused and driven."

INSIDE THE BATTING cage at Busch Stadium, Pujols' eyes narrow as he takes swing after perfect swing — and if one of them isn't perfect, he takes five extras. Pujols can't afford an imperfect stroke. There are standards to uphold here.

"Where he gets lots of respect is how hard he works," says Cardinals ace Adam Wainwright, who missed the 2011 season after undergoing Tommy John surgery. "He takes more swings in the cage than anyone. He's constantly doing film work. He knows the pitcher better than the pitcher knows himself. One thing I heard from Lance is that it's amazing to watch Albert throughout the whole season. He never gives up an at-bat. You're talking 162 games. I know how tough it is for me to grind out three at-bats. Not one of 600 from him."

The whole idea of work ethic isn't as tangible as consistency. Nobody logs practice swings, time spent in the cage, hours studying tendencies. Ballplayers are savvy, though, and know the difference between somebody who tries to look like he's working hard and somebody who strives for greatness.

"He doesn't have to work hard," pitcher Carlos Zambrano says. "He still does anyway."

Mozeliak once said Pujols could roll out of bed and hit .330. His first hitting coach, Mitchell Page, said Pujols' hands are "like lightning." His manager, Tony La Russa, admits, "Some people are just gifted." And yet, Pujols takes none of it for granted. He is motivated by equal parts fear and want. He hates that scouts once saw him

THE BEST EVER?

Through his first 11 seasons in the Major Leagues, Albert Pujols ranks sixth all time in on-base-plus-slugging percentage. Here's how his first 11 years stack up to the first 11 seasons (minimum 81 games per season) of the other players ranked in the top six in career OPS.

Player	AVG	OBP	SLG	OPS	HR	2B	RBI
Babe Ruth	.350	.486	.726	1.211	461	348	1,357
Ted Williams	.346	.485	.633	1.118	352	389	1,350
Lou Gehrig	.342	.446	.637	1.083	377	423	1,555
Jimmie Foxx	.335	.439	.639	1.077	426	337	1,495
Albert Pujols	**.328**	**.420**	**.617**	**1.037**	**445**	**455**	**1,329**
Barry Bonds	.288	.404	.548	.952	334	333	993

PUJOLS' FIRST HITTING COACH SAID HIS HANDS ARE "LIKE LIGHTNING." HIS MANAGER ADMITS, "SOME PEOPLE ARE JUST GIFTED." AND YET, PUJOLS TAKES NONE OF IT FOR GRANTED.

as a pudgy kid without a position, and he craves greatness. There is a reason that Pujols — a first-time free agent this winter — wants the biggest contract in sports: Being No. 2 is not something with which he's familiar.

So he locks himself inside the cage and tunes his swing like a piano. It's a marvel to watch: a ball coming every five seconds, the ensuing crack of the bat louder than anyone else's, on and on until his muscles memorize perfection.

"I want to see how he swings," Bryce Harper says. "What he does in BP, how he warms up."

Harper is just 19, the biggest phenom in a decade, and in his first spring camp, he'd already gotten the memo: When it comes to work, there is Pujols, and then there is everyone else.

ON JUNE 10, 2008, Pujols tore a calf muscle. The injury typically takes six weeks to heal. On June 26, Pujols returned to the Cardinals' lineup. He went 4 for 4.

Certainly the least recognized and appreciated of Pujols' attributes is his willingness to play through pain. For five years, he has played with a torn ulnar collateral ligament, which usually requires Tommy John surgery. He continues to put off the procedure, lest he have to sit out an entire season.

"He's tough," Texas Rangers reliever Mike Adams says. "You see that. You don't want to give hitters credit. You never do. But you have to with him. He works an at-bat like a guy half his size. He doesn't take a second off. You're never going to sneak something by him. He's got grit."

Though usually a word associated with the David Ecksteins of the game, grit does encapsulate Pujols well. He has been on the disabled list three times in his career — the third time coming this year, when he fractured his wrist while applying a tag and was supposed to miss six weeks but came back in fewer than three — and missed just 77 games total. By the end of a year, Pujols is so mummified in ice packs after games that he waddles instead of walks. Sure, he manages a smart diet and shuns alcohol, and yes, he exercises intensely year-round; but many other players with the same discipline can't fight through injuries. Pujols credits a higher being, and the only explanation is that he was blessed with a sick tolerance for pain.

"You blow your elbow out and it hurts," says Minnesota closer Joe Nathan, who suffered the same arm injury in 2010 and underwent Tommy John surgery. "It's not like you shake it off and go shopping that night. I don't know how anyone could play with one."

While Nathan's sentiment is well-intended, he forgot one thing: This is Albert Pujols, and what applies to everyone else really is of little pertinence.

Decade two got underway this year, and even if it's half as good as the first, Pujols will retire with his name etched next to Babe Ruth's, Ted Williams', Hank Aaron's, Lou Gehrig's and Willie Mays', knocking someone off the sport's Mount Rushmore.

"I honestly believe he's the best hitter in the history of the game," Berkman says. "Not just today. Ever. You can't show me a career that has started as well. You can talk about the old guys all you want. The pitching is better than ever. The talent pool is bigger than when Ruth and Williams played. You have specialists now — seventh-inning guys. Seventh inning!"

Before the season, Berkman reveled in the chance to see Pujols up close. He knew to expect some of the less glorious things — the tunnel-visioned Pujols, who, if shaken from his pregame routine, turns gruff — but they're a fair trade-off for beholding Pujols daily.

"He shoulders more today as a superstar than ever," Cardinals pitcher Kyle McClellan says. "And he does it better than anyone. He's focused. He's a leader. He's a special person, and he just happens to be an even better baseball player."

The greatest appreciation for Pujols came at the 2009 All-Star Game, which was as much an homage to Pujols as to the Midsummer Classic. Held in St. Louis, the festivities featured him in almost every capacity. He was the city's emissary to the game. He caught the first pitch from President Obama. He started at first base. If it weren't clear to Pujols how baseball felt about him to that point, it was thereafter.

"I appreciate it," Pujols said later that season, and it was unusual of him to let down his guard. Vulnerability is not among the traits he shows often, and yet it's essential to who he is. It drives all the other ones: The machine starts churning, and it supercharges his work ethic, and that pilots his consistency. With a little help from whatever injury gods do exist, he goes out every night and does things not seen for decades.

And from the plate to the mound to the stands and beyond, we all watch and appreciate, hypnotized by possibility. After all these years, Albert Pujols still has baseball entranced. We're not rushing to snap our fingers, either. ◆

Jeff Passan is a national baseball writer for Yahoo! Sports.

NOT WITHOUT A FIGHT

Although injuries to key players can seem devastating at the time, some teams don't let bad luck keep them from getting up off the mat.

By Jake Schwartzstein

The loss of Adam Wainwright was seen by many as too much for the Cardinals to overcome, but they regrouped and managed to win the World Series.

AS NATE SCHIERHOLTZ camped underneath a fly ball in shallow right-center field in the top of the 12th inning on May 25 and the Florida Marlins' Scott Cousins stood on third base anxiously awaiting his chance to tag up and score, San Francisco Giants star catcher Buster Posey flipped off his mask and prepared for the incoming play at the plate. Schierholtz unleashed a bullet — a near-perfect, one-hop throw to Posey. The roar of the crowd intensified.

But upon attempting to corral the baseball — which he ultimately couldn't handle — while simultaneously blocking the plate and turning to try to tag the runner, Posey was bulldozed by the 195-pound force of Cousins coming full tilt. Catapulted back, the catcher's lower left

leg got caught beneath him at an angle that required zero medical expertise to see was unnatural. It was a clean play with an unclean result, and as Posey writhed on the ground, the park fell silent, like someone had hit the mute button on the TV.

A minute or so passed with the backstop being tended to before a nervous chant of "Po-sey! Po-sey!" broke out among fans. A beloved figure in San Francisco, it was as if Giants faithful were begging for a miracle.

They did not get one. Posey gingerly hopped on one leg back to the Giants' dugout with the assistance of the medical staff, not to return for the rest of the season. The young but mature catcher, a key figure in the club's 2010

title run, would require surgery after breaking his fibula and tearing ligaments in his ankle.

"I thought it was bad," says Giants pitcher Matt Cain of the injury. "I was just hoping he was going to be alright."

Following the game — which the Giants lost, 7-6 — the reigning world champions sat in first place with a 2.5-game lead in the National League West, but at 27-21, they weren't exactly running away with the division. When Posey hobbled into the clubhouse, it would have been understandable if Giants fans thought their team would completely fall out of the pennant race. After all, this was the best hitter on a 2010 team with an average offense, a guy who won the Rookie of the Year Award and who, in 2011, had entrenched himself in the cleanup spot for a lineup that was again struggling to score runs. The future of the Giants in '11 — two months from acquiring star outfielder Carlos Beltran — didn't look bright.

Of course, the Giants weren't alone in their misfortune. The Rangers lost 2010 AL MVP Josh Hamilton for nearly six weeks; the Brewers played the first month without newly acquired pitcher and former Cy Young Award winner Zack Greinke; the Rays lost third baseman Evan Longoria for more than a month; and the Phillies were without Chase Utley until May 23. But the team that could most empathize with the Giants was St. Louis, which suffered its big loss long before the season began, when ace Adam Wainwright underwent season-ending Tommy John surgery in February. To top it off, the Cardinals had to face the prospect of three-time MVP Albert Pujols missing at least six weeks when he fractured his wrist on June 19. Fortunately for them, he returned in less than three.

BUT AS PROFESSIONALS are wont to do, players on these teams didn't dwell on their bad luck. Rather, they kept on winning. The Rangers, though just one game over .500 when Hamilton returned on May 23, still had a hold on first place in the AL West at that point. The Rays, meanwhile, lost their first four games without Longoria but finished April on a 15-6 run before he returned on May 3. Milwaukee, too, survived Greinke's absence with a 13-12 April mark. And the Phillies were so loaded with talent — featuring the Big Four of Cliff Lee, Roy Halladay, Roy Oswalt and Cole Hamels, as well as Ryan Howard in the lineup — that they still blew away the competition, going 28-18 before their second baseman returned.

In the case of the Giants, they soon started winning at a better pace than they had before Posey's injury.

"Knowing Posey was gone was a tough blow, but guys know there is no reason to throw in the towel," says Giants relief pitcher Javier Lopez.

"We knew the situation. We knew what we had to do," Aubrey Huff adds.

After a brief slide dropped San Francisco to second place at the end of May, the Giants rebounded in June with a 10-4 run in the month's first two weeks. The club would go 17-11 in June, good for a .607 winning percentage and a better record than it had in either of the season's first two months.

"If you would have told me that before [the injury] happened, I wouldn't have believed it," Cain says about their improved record. "Posey's such a big key to the group."

Similarly, the Cardinals couldn't waste time feeling sorry for themselves. Sure, Wainwright had been among the best pitchers in the Major Leagues over the past two years, finishing third in NL Cy Young Award voting in 2009 and second in '10. But the Cardinals still went into the season with possibly the best offensive 1-2 punch in the Majors in Pujols and Matt Holliday, and they featured 2005 Cy Young Award winner Chris Carpenter. And while no Cardinal was pleased upon hearing Wainwright's diagnosis, at least it happened early.

"For the team, it was almost better that it happened when it did because we had all of Spring Training to deal with it," says Lance Berkman, who just finished his first season as a Cardinal. "We still have Carpenter, still have Jaime Garcia, so our mentality was, 'Let's go get 'em.'"

No Cardinal went out and got 'em this year quite like Berkman. At age 35 and coming off his least productive season in the Majors since he was 23, Berkman signed a relatively modest one-year contract last winter — and turned out to be the best bargain of the offseason. Making his first All-Star team since 2008, the Big Puma finished with 31 homers, 23 doubles and a .959 OPS on the season.

"It's like Berkman replaced Wainwright," says Reds All-Star Joey Votto.

Typically, the Giants have kept an edge due to pitching. Their staff has been one of the best the past three years thanks to All-Stars Cain, Tim Lincecum and closer Brian Wilson and a bevy of other talented arms in Madison Bumgarner and relievers Jeremy Affeldt, Sergio Romo and Lopez. Don't forget starter Ryan Vogelsong, a 34-year-old righty who should be getting his own docudrama offer from Disney any day now. After returning to The Show following a five-year absence, he made the All-Star team

A resurgent season from Lance Berkman in his first year with the Cardinals helped the team put up the most runs in the National League in 2011.

and was fourth in the National League in ERA (2.71) by season's end. Only the Phillies' staff allowed fewer runs than the Giants' in 2011.

"It was pitching. Pitching and defense," Huff says about the Giants' performance this year. "We just found a way late in games. You can't explain it any more than that. I'd put our pitching and bullpen against anyone in baseball."

Indeed, while San Francisco's rotation was superb, the team's negative-8 run differential — despite finishing 10 games over .500 (86-76) — indicated an impressive showing by the bullpen. With 66 save chances on the year, the 'pen had to repeatedly work in high leverage situations. Other good indicators of its dominance? How about a .223 batting average against, .631 OPS against, 26 wins, .591 winning percentage and 3.04 ERA.

Considering the praise Posey has received for leading the staff, it's a testament to his replacements, Eli Whiteside and Chris Stewart, that there wasn't a noticeable drop-off in runs allowed — really, no drop-off at all. The 31-year-old Whiteside, who suddenly became the regular backstop, hadn't played more than 56 Big League games in a season before 2011, while Stewart — at 29 — hadn't participated in more than 17. But the pitching staff's ERA actually improved after these two took the reigns, with a 3.03 mark in June, 2.97 in July and 3.08 in August before a September "swoon" in which it had a mark of 3.61 — compared to 3.53 in April and 3.09 in May.

"Whiteside was great; he was a calming force," Lopez says. "He's not frightened by the stage. Stewart is a good defender who controls the running game."

Losing Buster Posey's bat was a big blow to the Giants, but behind their strong pitching staff, they still managed to contend for much of the season.

In Adam Wainwright's absence, Jaime Garcia emerged as a leader on the Cardinals' staff.

WITH PUJOLS, HOLLIDAY and Berkman, it's hardly shocking that the Cardinals finished the season with a National League–high 762 runs scored. What is somewhat surprising is that they can also give thanks to their pitchers for the team's postseason berth and, ultimately, its World Series championship. With assistance from pitching coach Dave Duncan, St. Louis put together a solid rotation that included Carpenter, Garcia and Kyle Lohse, as well as 2009 All-Star Edwin Jackson, acquired in July.

Coming off his most difficult season a year ago, when he went 4-8 with a career-worst 6.55 ERA, the 32-year-old Lohse looked to come back strong in 2011. The righty did just that, surpassing his marks from last year in wins, innings pitched and strikeouts by mid-July and cutting his ERA nearly in half, down to 3.39 by year's end. The 25-year-old Garcia, meanwhile, stepped into a leadership role in just his second full season in the Bigs. He finished second on the team in wins (13), third in ERA (3.56) and second in K/BB (3.12).

While the starting rotation is to be commended for the performances it had this year, the bullpen cannot be forgotten. GM John Mozeliak made key pickups midseason by acquiring Octavio Dotel and Marc Rzepczynski from the Blue Jays. Dotel recorded a 3.28 ERA and two saves in 29 games for the Cardinals, and both he and Rzepczynski excelled in the postseason. Another bullpen arm who developed into a big-time pitcher was Jason Motte, who took over the closer's role in August and ran with it, almost making it look easy come October.

While each of these pitchers deserves praise for the work he put in and the team's subsequent success, it doesn't hurt to have Duncan as a tutor. Resurrecting careers and getting the most out of his pupils is kind of his thing, and the Cardinals knew they could still churn out a quality rotation even without their most important piece, a point that wasn't lost on the team's batters.

"There is definitely a comfort level with Dave as our pitching coach," Holliday says. "You do go, 'Aw, man, we lost Wainwright,' but we had options, so there was comfort knowing Dunc could ease that blow."

Going into any season, one goal every team has is to stay healthy, but that objective is rarely met. Teams like the Giants, Cardinals, Rays, Rangers and Phillies, though, know that opponents won't take pity on them. Injuries occur in sports. Losers whine about them; championship-caliber teams overcome them. The only thing left to do is play on and win despite depletions to the regular roster.

"Things happen," says Giants skipper Bruce Bochy. "What's important is how you handle it. Guys moved on."

Watching these teams show the mettle to continue their success — and in the Cardinals' case, win the whole thing — makes it all the more intriguing. ◆

Jake Schwartzstein is a project editor for Major League Baseball Properties.

MINOR LEAGUE
RESULTS

AAA MEMPHIS REDBIRDS (77-66)
2nd in PCL American Northern Division

AA SPRINGFIELD CARDINALS (62-78)
4th in Texas League North Division

HIGH-A PALM BEACH CARDINALS (68-70)
3rd in Florida State League South Division

A QUAD CITIES RIVER BANDITS (81-56)
1st in Midwest League Western Division
Swept Lansing Lugnuts to win the championship

MAJOR LEAGUE BASEBALL PROPERTIES

Senior Vice President, Consumer Products	HOWARD SMITH
Vice President, Publishing	DONALD S. HINTZE
Editorial Director	MIKE McCORMICK
Publications Art Director	FAITH M. RITTENBERG
Senior Production Manager	CLAIRE WALSH
Managing Editor	JON SCHWARTZ
Account Executive, Publishing	CHRIS RODDAY
Senior Publishing Coordinator	ANAMIKA PANCHOO
Associate Art Director	MARK CALIMBAS
Project Editor	JAKE SCHWARTZSTEIN
Project Assistant Editors	PAUL BOYE
	ALLISON DUFFY
Editorial Intern	NICK CARROLL

MAJOR LEAGUE BASEBALL PHOTOS

Director	RICH PILLING
Photo Editor	JESSICA FOSTER
World Series Asst. Photo Editors	MATTHEW KUTZ
	ANJA SCHLEIN

THE McCLELLAND & STEWART/FENN TEAM
JORDAN FENN
ELIZABETH KRIBS
MICHAEL MELGAARD
JAMES YOUNG, RUTA LIORMONAS
JANINE LAPORTE